LEARN SOLIDITY

*From Fundamentals to Practical
Applications With AI Virtual Tutoring*

Diego Rodrigues

StudioD21

LEARN SOLIDITY
From Fundamentals to Practical Applications
With AI Virtual Tutoring

2025 Edition
Author: Diego Rodrigues

Published by StudioD21.

Important Note

The codes and scripts presented in this book aim to illustrate the concepts discussed in the chapters, serving as practical examples. These examples were developed in custom, controlled environments, and therefore there is no guarantee that they will work fully in all scenarios. It is essential to check the configurations and customizations of the environment where they will be applied to ensure their proper functioning. We thank you for your understanding.

CONTENTS

TECHNOLOGICAL INNOVATION

**Exclusive Access to AI-Assisted Virtual
Tutoring: D21 Reader Bonus**

**AILearning Experience — Learn with an
Agent, Advance with Purpose**

The AILearning Experience redefines the traditional structure of
education. Instead of consuming content linearly and passively,
the reader is invited to interact with an intelligent textual
system that responds with technical precision, guides decision-
making, and promotes learning through trial, error, and
improvement.

You learn by doing, solving, and asking — not just by watching
or memorizing.

Access the Demonstration Version for Free

Seven Core Principles of the AILearning Experience

1. Simulated Tutoring with Visible Technical Progress
Learners can see their own growth through the increasing complexity of tasks completed with AI Agent support.

2. Cognitive Microchains
Each answer opens a decision path: the user can go deeper, explore variations, or take on new technical challenges in real time.

3. Text-Guided Execution
No clicks, videos, or software needed. All learning is guided by clear technical instructions and hands-on simulations focused on real application.

4. Memory-Free, Yet Perceptive Adaptation
The agent does not retain session history, but simulates pattern recognition, adjusting answers based on question type, vocabulary, and phrasing.

5. Technical Challenges with Hidden Validation
The agent analyzes user responses to proposed tests and simulations to assess learning and suggest the next step.

6. Functional, Not Decorative Responses
All answers have a clear technical purpose. Language is precise, instructive, and free of unnecessary narrative or repetition.

7. Multilingual Operation with Controlled Scope
The experience is fully available in:

Português · English · Español · Français · Deutsch · Italiano · العربية
· 中文 · हिंदी · 日本語 ·   ·
Türkçe · Русский,
with full didactic consistency and technical rigor.

Operational Purpose

Teach through application. Guide through challenge. Validate through practice.

QR CODE AND ACTIVATION LINK

In this chapter, you will find the QR code and activation link to access your embedded AI Agent.
This tool will accompany your learning journey and adapt to your progress with real-time feedback and challenge-based guidance.

May this experience be not only helpful — but truly transformative.
Continue forward with confidence.

GREETINGS!

Hello, dear reader!

It is with great pleasure that I welcome you, who has decided to embark on a fascinating journey through the universe of programming in Solidity, the language behind smart contracts and one of the most influential pillars in the blockchain ecosystem. Your choice to explore this topic demonstrates an admirable commitment to innovation, continuous learning and building technological solutions that are transforming the digital future.

Solidity is not just a programming language; it is the key to creating decentralized applications that redefine how we interact, transact and trust. Through smart contracts, it allows you to automate processes, eliminate intermediaries and provide security in an increasingly connected world. Mastering Solidity is being at the forefront of the blockchain revolution, a field full of opportunities for visionary developers.

In this book, you will find a structured and practical approach, which will guide you from the essential fundamentals of the language to the implementation of real and complex projects. Each chapter is designed to provide accessible and progressive learning, combining solid theoretical concepts with practical examples that consolidate your understanding and confidence in applying knowledge.

It doesn't matter if you're just starting out, exploring new possibilities as a developer, or looking to improve your skills to work on projects with global impact. This guide has been carefully crafted to meet the needs of all experience levels, ensuring you feel challenged and inspired at every step.

We live in a unique time where blockchain technology is reshaping entire industries, and Solidity is the tool that enables these changes. Whether developing smart contracts for decentralized finance (DeFi), non-fungible tokens (NFTs), or innovative solutions for industry, mastering this language offers a direct path to global market leadership.

This book is more than a manual; It is an invitation to transform ideas into reality. Throughout the pages, you will find up-to-date knowledge, secure development practices, and thought-provoking challenges that will enable you to design and implement robust and efficient decentralized applications.

Are you ready to explore the world of Solidity, unleash your creative potential and build solutions that will impact the future? Let's start this transformative journey together and unlock the true power of smart contracts!

Welcome to this innovative learning experience. Your evolution begins now.

ABOUT THE AUTHOR

www.linkedin.com/in/diegoexpertai

Best-Selling Author, Diego Rodrigues is an International Consultant and Writer specializing in Market Intelligence, Technology and Innovation. With 42 international certifications from institutions such as IBM, Google, Microsoft, AWS, Cisco, and Boston University, Ec-Council, Palo Alto and META.

Rodrigues is an expert in Artificial Intelligence, Machine Learning, Data Science, Big Data, Blockchain, Connectivity Technologies, Ethical Hacking and Threat Intelligence.

Since 2003, Rodrigues has developed more than 200 projects for important brands in Brazil, USA and Mexico. In 2024, he consolidates himself as one of the largest new generation authors of technical books in the world, with more than 180 titles published in six languages.

PRESENTATION OF THE BOOK

Welcome to **LEARN SOLIDITY: From Fundamentals to Practical Applications**!

We are excited to have you join us on this transformative journey through the world of Solidity programming. If you are reading this introduction, it is because you have already recognized the revolutionary impact of blockchain and realized that Solidity is the essential tool for unlocking the potential of smart contracts. This book has been carefully designed to be a comprehensive guide, offering a clear path from the essential fundamentals to the most advanced practical applications.

Solidity programming is a game changer in the development of decentralized applications (dApps). Through it, it is possible to automate processes, build secure solutions and create applications that transform industries. This book was structured to enable you to master this language and apply it in a practical and strategic way, opening doors to new opportunities in the technology market.

Combining well-founded theory and detailed practical examples, this guide caters to beginners and experienced developers alike. Each chapter is designed to ensure that you not only understand the concepts, but also know how to apply them in real-world scenarios, creating robust and impactful solutions.

Book Structure

In the following chapters, we will explore Solidity in a progressive and structured way, dividing learning into clear steps. Here's a summary of what you'll find:

- **Chapter 1.** Introduction to Solidity
  Overview of the language and its importance in the blockchain ecosystem.
- **Chapter 2.** Development Environment Configuration
  Installation of tools such as Remix, Truffle and Hardhat.
- **Chapter 3.** Solidity Fundamentals
  Basic structure of a smart contract, data types and variables.
- **Chapter 4.** Functions in Solidity
  Creation of functions and good development practices.
- **Chapter 5.** Flow Control and Loops
  Use of conditional structures and loops in contract logic.
- **Chapter 6.** Events and Logs
  Recording events on the blockchain for tracking.
- **Chapter 7.** Arrays and Mappings
  Fundamental data structures for Solidity.
- **Chapter 8.** Structures and Enums
  Creation and use of custom structures and enums.
- **Chapter 9.** Modifiers and Inheritance
  Code reuse with inheritance and control of functions with modifiers.
- **Chapter 10.** Payments and Transfers
  Ether handling and transaction security.
- **Chapter 11.** Security in Smart Contracts
  Vulnerability protection and best practices.
- **Chapter 12.** Testing Contracts
  Use of frameworks to ensure reliability.
- **Chapter 13.** Contract Deployment
  Deployment process on test networks and mainnets.
- **Chapter 14.** Interaction with dApps
  Connection of contracts with frontend interfaces using libraries.
- **Chapter 15.** ERC-20: Creating Fungible Tokens

Implementation of the ERC-20 standard for tokens.
- **Chapter 16.** ERC-721: Creating NFTs
  Development of non-fungible tokens and their uses.
- **Chapter 17.** ERC-1155: Multimodality Tokens
  Creation of fungible and non-fungible tokens in a single contract.
- **Chapter 18.** Complex Contracts and DAO
  Development of robust decentralized systems.
- **Chapter 19.** Contract Interoperability
  Communication between different smart contracts.
- **Chapter 20.** Gas Optimization
  Strategies to reduce execution costs.
- **Chapter 21.** Staking Contracts
  Implementation of rewards and staking systems.
- **Chapter 22.** Real Use Cases
  Practical examples of smart contracts in operation.
- **Chapter 23.** Futuro do Solidity
  Emerging trends and innovations in language.
- **Chapter 24.** Complete Practical Example
  A functional project from beginning to completion.
- **Chapter 25.** Advanced Tips and Resources
  Best practices and communities for continuous learning.

Now that you have an overview of what this book offers, we invite you to dive into this learning and master Solidity. At the end of this journey, you will be empowered to create innovative solutions and make an impact in the digital world. We look forward to sharing this path with you!

CHAPTER 1. INTRODUCTION TO SOLIDITY

Solidity is a contract-oriented programming language specifically designed to create smart contracts that run on the Ethereum Virtual Machine (EVM). This language plays a crucial role in the blockchain ecosystem, enabling the creation of robust, secure and scalable decentralized applications (dApps). Solidity is essential for developing solutions that eliminate intermediaries, increase efficiency and promote transparency in various sectors.

The rise of Solidity is closely linked to the growth of Ethereum, the blockchain platform that introduced smart contracts. Unlike traditional blockchains, which focus exclusively on recording transactions, Ethereum allows the execution of programmable code. Solidity was designed to take advantage of this capability, providing an accessible syntax and advanced features that enable the creation of versatile smart contracts.

The language was inspired by languages like JavaScript, Python, and C++, making it familiar to experienced developers. Its learning curve, combined with its practical application in blockchain, makes it a preferred choice for beginners and professionals alike. Solidity empowers developers to implement everything from simple functions, such as token transfers, to complex systems, such as decentralized finance platforms (DeFi) and Decentralized Autonomous Organizations (DAOs).

The main feature of Solidity is its contract orientation. Each contract is a unit of code that encapsulates data and functions.

This allows for modular and organized programming, facilitating the creation, testing and maintenance of decentralized applications. A smart contract, in essence, is a self-executing agreement with terms defined in code. It operates in a transparent and immutable manner, ensuring that the parties involved comply with the terms without the need for mutual trust.

The Ethereum Virtual Machine, where Solidity contracts are executed, is a decentralized virtual machine that processes transactions and maintains the integrity of the blockchain. All contracts implemented in EVM follow the same rules, ensuring consistency and security. EVM's decentralization means that the code runs on thousands of nodes on the Ethereum network, making it resistant to censorship and attacks.

Creating smart contracts in Solidity starts with defining a basic contract. Consider the following example of a contract that stores and retrieves a message:

solidity

```solidity
// SPDX-License-Identifier: MIT
pragma solidity ^0.8.0;

contract SimpleStorage {
    string private message;

    function setMessage(string memory _message) public {
        message = _message;
    }

    function getMessage() public view returns (string memory) {
        return message;
    }
}
```

This contract exemplifies the fundamentals of Solidity. It

contains a state variable message, which stores data on the blockchain, and two functions: setMessage to set the value and getMessage to get it back. The function setMessage is marked as public, allowing any user to interact with it, while getMessage It is a reading function that does not consume gas, as it does not change the status of the contract.

The keyword pragma indicates the version of the Solidity compiler that should be used. Specifying the version ensures that the code is compatible with future compiler updates. The keyword memory, used in function arguments, indicates that the variable exists temporarily during function execution, while storage refers to persistent variables.

Solidity also supports varied data types such as integers, booleans, and custom structures. This allows you to create smart contracts that handle complex data and implement advanced logic. Below is an example contract that manages a user registry:

solidity

```
// SPDX-License-Identifier: MIT
pragma solidity ^0.8.0;

contract UserRegistry {
    struct User {
        string name;
        uint age;
        bool isActive;
    }

    mapping(address => User) private users;

    function registerUser(string memory _name, uint _age)
public {
        require(_age > 0, "Age must be greater than zero");
        users[msg.sender] = User(_name, _age, true);
```

```
    }

    function getUser(address _userAddress) public view returns
(string memory, uint, bool) {
        User memory user = users[_userAddress];
        return (user.name, user.age, user.isActive);
    }

    function deactivateUser() public {
        require(users[msg.sender].isActive, "User already
inactive");
        users[msg.sender].isActive = false;
    }
}
```

The example above uses a structure (struct) to represent users and a mapping (mapping) to associate each address with a user. The contract includes validations with the keyword require, which stops execution if a condition is not met, protecting the contract against invalid inputs.

Another important aspect of Solidity is the interaction with Ether, Ethereum's native cryptocurrency. Smart contracts can send and receive Ether, enabling the creation of decentralized financial systems. The following example demonstrates how to implement a simple wallet contract:

solidity

```
// SPDX-License-Identifier: MIT
pragma solidity ^0.8.0;

contract SimpleWallet {
    address private owner;

    constructor() {
        owner = msg.sender;
    }
```

```solidity
    receive() external payable {}

    function withdraw(uint _amount) public {
        require(msg.sender == owner, "Only the owner can
withdraw funds");
        require(address(this).balance >= _amount, "Insufficient
balance");
        payable(owner).transfer(_amount);
    }

    function getBalance() public view returns (uint) {
        return address(this).balance;
    }
}
```

The above contract defines a wallet that allows the owner to deposit Ether and withdraw amounts. The special function receive is triggered whenever Ether is sent directly to the contract. The keyword payable is used to indicate that a function can receive or send Ether.

Security is a critical aspect in developing smart contracts. Solidity provides mechanisms to protect contracts against attacks, such as strict validations and secure design patterns. It is essential to avoid practices such as reliance on untrusted external data and inappropriate manipulation of Ether values.

Furthermore, gas consumption, which represents the computational cost of executing smart contracts, must be carefully managed. Well-optimized contracts not only reduce costs for users, but also increase overall network efficiency.

Learning Solidity is an essential step for any developer interested in exploring the potential of blockchain. The language offers powerful tools for turning ideas into reality, creating decentralized applications that are secure, scalable and efficient. Mastering Solidity opens doors to contribute to innovative projects in areas such as finance, healthcare, governance and more, shaping the future of the blockchain ecosystem.

CHAPTER 2. CONFIGURING THE DEVELOPMENT ENVIRONMENT

Efficient development in Solidity requires a well-configured working environment that supports the creation, testing, and deployment of smart contracts. Configuring the appropriate tools not only streamlines the development process, but also reduces errors and increases productivity. Among the essential tools for working with Solidity are Remix, Truffle and Hardhat, each with specific characteristics that meet different needs in the development cycle. With these tools, it is possible to write, compile, test and deploy smart contracts in a practical and reliable way.

The first step in setting up the environment is to install prerequisites, such as Node.js, a platform that manages dependencies and allows you to run JavaScript-based development tools. Node.js can be downloaded and installed from its official website. Additionally, it is important to install the npm package manager, which comes with Node.js, or use Yarn, a widely used alternative.

After configuring these fundamental components, the next step is to choose the development tool. Remix is ideal for beginners as it offers a user-friendly web-based interface, while Truffle and Hardhat are more suitable for advanced projects, providing detailed control over the development cycle.

Configuring Remix

Remix is a browser-based IDE that allows you to write, compile and test smart contracts directly on the web. You don't need to install any additional software to start using Remix, making it accessible to developers of all skill levels. To access Remix, simply open https://remix.ethereum.org in a compatible browser.

From the main Remix panel, you can create new files for your contracts and organize them into directories. The code editor supports syntax highlighting, auto-suggestions, and error detection. The built-in compiler allows you to check syntax and compile smart contracts quickly. Additionally, Remix includes a blockchain simulator, called a "JavaScript VM" environment, that makes it easy to test contracts without the need for an external network.

To create and test a contract in Remix, start by creating a file with the extension .sun. In the editor, write a simple contract:

solidity

```solidity
// SPDX-License-Identifier: MIT
pragma solidity ^0.8.0;

contract Counter {
    uint public count;

    function increment() public {
        count += 1;
    }

    function decrement() public {
        require(count > 0, "Count cannot be negative");
        count -= 1;
    }
}
```

After writing the code, select the compiler in the Remix side tab and choose the version corresponding to the pragma specified in the contract. Compile the contract to check for errors. Then, use the blockchain simulator to deploy and interact with the contract, testing its functionality.

Installing and Configuring Truffle

Truffle is an advanced framework that facilitates the development of smart contracts, offering features for project management, automated testing, and deployment. To install Truffle, use npm or Yarn:

bash

```
npm install -g truffle
```

After installation, create a new project by running the command:

bash

```
truffle heat
```

Truffle organizes the project into predefined directories. The folder contracts contains the smart contracts, migrations stores the deployment scripts and test is used for testing. Create a contract in the folder contracts and add the following code:

solidity

```
// SPDX-License-Identifier: MIT
pragma solidity ^0.8.0;

contract Greeter {
    string private greeting;

    constructor(string memory _greeting) {
        greeting = _greeting;
    }
```

```solidity
    function greet() public view returns (string memory) {
        return greeting;
    }

    function setGreeting(string memory _newGreeting) public {
        greeting = _newGreeting;
    }
}
```

After creating the contract, update the migration file in the folder migrations to add the newly created contract:

javascript

```javascript
const Greeter = artifacts.require("Greeter");

module.exports = function (deployer) {
  deployer.deploy(Greeter, "Hello, Solidity!");
};
```

To test the contract, create a test script in the folder test using JavaScript. A simple example of testing with the Chai library would be:

javascript

```javascript
const Greeter = artifacts.require("Greeter");

contract("Greeter", (accounts) => {
  it("should return the initial greeting", async () => {
    const instance = await Greeter.deployed();
    const greeting = await instance.greet();
    assert.equal(greeting, "Hello, Solidity!", "Initial greeting does
not match");
  });

  it("should update the greeting", async () => {
```

```
  const instance = await Greeter.deployed();
  await instance.setGreeting("New Greeting");
  const updatedGreeting = await instance.greet();
  assert.equal(updatedGreeting, "New Greeting", "Greeting was
not updated correctly");
  });
});
```

To run the tests, use the command:

bash

```
truffle test
```

Truffle makes it easy to execute contracts on testnets or mainnet. Be sure to set up a provider like Infura or Alchemy and a wallet like MetaMask to manage private keys.

Configuring and Using Hardhat

Hardhat is a modern and flexible tool for developing smart contracts. It allows you to run tests, deploy contracts, and debug errors with ease. Install Hardhat using npm:

bash

```
npm install --save-dev hardhat
```

Create a Hardhat project with the command:

bash

```
npx hardhat
```

Choose the option to create a basic project and follow the instructions to configure the environment. Hardhat uses plugins to extend its functionality. One of the most popular plugins is @nomiclabs/hardhat-ethers, which makes it easy to interact with contracts using the Ethers.js library. Install the plugin with:

bash

```
npm install --save-dev @nomiclabs/hardhat-ethers ethers
```

Add the following contract to the directory contracts:

solidity

```solidity
// SPDX-License-Identifier: MIT
pragma solidity ^0.8.0;

contract Token {
    string public name = "Hardhat Token";
    string public symbol = "HHT";
    uint8 public decimals = 18;
    uint public totalSupply = 1000000 * (10 ** uint(decimals));
    mapping(address => uint) public balanceOf;

    constructor() {
        balanceOf[msg.sender] = totalSupply;
    }

    function transfer(address _to, uint _value) public returns (bool success) {
        require(balanceOf[msg.sender] >= _value, "Insufficient balance");
        balanceOf[msg.sender] -= _value;
        balanceOf[_to] += _value;
        return true;
    }
}
```

To test the contract, create a test file in the directory test:

javascript

```javascript
const { expect } = require("chai");

describe("Token Contract", () => {
  let Token, token, owner, addr1;

  beforeEach(async () => {
    Token = await ethers.getContractFactory("Token");
    [owner, addr1] = await ethers.getSigners();
    token = await Token.deploy();
    await token.deployed();
  });

  it("should assign the total supply to the owner", async () => {
    const ownerBalance = await token.balanceOf(owner.address);
    expect(await token.totalSupply()).to.equal(ownerBalance);
  });

  it("should transfer tokens between accounts", async () => {
    await token.transfer(addr1.address, 100);
    expect(await token.balanceOf(addr1.address)).to.equal(100);
  });
});
```

Run the tests with:

bash

```bash
npx hardhat test
```

Hardhat also supports transaction debugging, making it easier to identify and fix issues in smart contracts.

Setting up an efficient development environment in Solidity allows developers to create, test, and deploy smart contracts in a structured way. With tools such as Remix, Truffle and Hardhat, it is possible to manage projects of different levels of complexity, ensuring a productive workflow and reliable results.

CHAPTER 3. FUNDAMENTALS OF SOLIDITY

Solidity is a programming language created to build smart contracts that run on the Ethereum Virtual Machine (EVM). Understanding its basic structure, data types, variables, and visibility modifiers is essential to creating secure, efficient, and reusable contracts. This chapter explores the fundamentals of Solidity, detailing how primary elements of the language combine to form robust smart contracts.

A contract in Solidity is a unit of code that contains data and functions. It acts as a self-sufficient program that manages interactions and stores information on the blockchain. Understanding how contracts are structured and work is crucial for any developer in the Ethereum ecosystem.

The creation of contracts begins with the declaration of a pragma, which defines the version of the Solidity compiler used. This ensures that the contract is compiled with the appropriate version, preventing future inconsistencies. The basic structure of a contract includes definitions of state variables, functions, and optionally events and modifiers.

solidity

```
// SPDX-License-Identifier: MIT
pragma solidity ^0.8.0;

contract BasicContract {
    string public name;
```

```
constructor(string memory _name) {
    name = _name;
}

function setName(string memory _newName) public {
    name = _newName;
}

function getName() public view returns (string memory) {
    return name;
}
}
```

In the example above, the contract stores a variable name and provides functions to set and retrieve it. The keyword public makes the variable and functions accessible to anyone. The function constructor initializes the contract at the time of its deployment, while view specifies that a function does not change the state of the contract and is used to read data.

Data Types in Solidity

Smart contracts require the use of various types of data to handle different scenarios. Solidity supports simple types like integers, booleans, and strings, as well as compound types like arrays and mappings.

Integers

Solidity supports both signed and unsigned integers. The unsigned integers (uint) are used for non-negative values, while signed integers (int) allow positive and negative values. The default size is 256 bits, but can be adjusted in 8-bit increments, such as uint8 or int128.

solidity

```
uint public age = 25;
int public temperature = -10;

function setAge(uint _age) public {
    age = _age;
}
```

Not code, age is an unsigned integer that stores age, while temperature represents negative or positive values. Validation of values must be done to avoid invalid entries.

Booleanos

Boolean values (bool) are used to store true (true) or false (false). They are often used in conditions and checks.

solidity

```
bool public isActive;

function activate() public {
    isActive = true;
}

function deactivate() public {
    isActive = false;
}
```

In this case, isActive is used to indicate the state of the contract, which can be changed by specific roles.

Strings

Strings store text and are widely used for information such as names and messages. Strings in Solidity are manipulated in a limited way, but can be combined with other libraries for greater flexibility.

solidity

```solidity
string public greeting = "Hello, Blockchain!";

function setGreeting(string memory _newGreeting) public {
    greeting = _newGreeting;
}

function getGreeting() public view returns (string memory) {
    return greeting;
}
```

The keyword memory specifies that the string exists only during function execution. Strings stored on the blockchain use persistent storage space.

Arrays

Arrays are collections of elements of the same type, which can be fixed or dynamic in size. Fixed arrays have a set number of elements, while dynamic arrays can grow or shrink.

solidity

```solidity
uint[] public numbers;

function addNumber(uint _number) public {
    numbers.push(_number);
}

function getNumber(uint _index) public view returns (uint) {
    return numbers[_index];
```

```
}
```

In the example, the dynamic array numbers stores integers and allows adding new elements with the function push. The function getNumber retrieves a specific element based on the given index.

Mappings

Mappings are used to associate keys with values. They function like dictionaries and are useful for storing relationships such as account balances.

solidity

```
mapping(address => uint) public balances;

function deposit() public payable {
    balances[msg.sender] += msg.value;
}

function withdraw(uint _amount) public {
    require(balances[msg.sender] >= _amount, "Insufficient
balance");
    balances[msg.sender] -= _amount;
    payable(msg.sender).transfer(_amount);
}
```

In this contract, balances stores the balance of each address. The functions allow deposits and withdrawals, validating the balance before making transfers.

Visibility Modifiers

Visibility modifiers control access to functions and variables. Solidity offers four main levels of visibility:

- public: Access allowed to anyone.
- private: Restricted access to the contract itself.
- internal: Access allowed to the contract and its derivatives.
- external: Access permitted only by external calls.

solidity

```solidity
contract VisibilityExample {
    string public publicData = "Accessible by anyone";
    string private privateData = "Accessible only within
contract";

    function getPrivateData() public view returns (string
memory) {
        return privateData;
    }
}
```

In this case, publicData is publicly accessible, while privateData can only be accessed through internal functions.

Role Modifiers

Function modifiers add conditional logic before or after the main function executes. They are used to validate conditions, check permissions, and optimize code.

solidity

```solidity
contract ModifierExample {
    address private owner;

    modifier onlyOwner() {
        require(msg.sender == owner, "Caller is not the owner");
        _;
    }
```

```
constructor() {
    owner = msg.sender;
}

function restrictedAction() public onlyOwner {
    // Logic restricted to the owner
}
}
```

The modifier onlyOwner checks whether the function was called by the contract owner. The operator _ indicates where execution of the original function should continue after validation.

Events

Events allow you to record information on the blockchain so that external applications can monitor changes to the state of the contract.

solidity

```
contract EventExample {
    event ValueSet(uint value);

    uint public storedValue;

    function setValue(uint _value) public {
        storedValue = _value;
        emit ValueSet(_value);
    }
}
```

The function setValue records the new value set in an event, which can be read by applications that interact with the contract.

Good Practices in Solidity

Smart contract design requires attention to aspects such as security, efficiency and readability. The use of rigorous validations with require and assert, limiting unnecessary access and optimizing gas consumption are essential to guarantee reliable contracts.

Understanding the fundamentals of Solidity is the foundation for building efficient and secure smart contracts. Mastering the basic structure, data types and visibility modifiers allows you to create flexible and reliable solutions, opening up infinite possibilities in the blockchain ecosystem. Each element presented is an integral part of Solidity development, offering the necessary tools to face challenges and build innovations in the decentralized world.

CHAPTER 4. FUNCTIONS IN SOLIDITY

Functions are the basis for implementing logic in smart contracts in Solidity. They allow the execution of specific actions, manipulate stored data and interact with other contracts. Understanding the creation, structure, and types of roles, as well as implementation best practices, is essential to building efficient, secure, and scalable contracts.

Functions in Solidity follow a clear structure and can be customized with visibility modifiers and keywords that define behavior. Correct use of these characteristics helps to avoid errors and vulnerabilities, in addition to optimizing the performance of smart contracts.

Basic Structure of a Function

A function in Solidity is composed of a header and a body. The header defines the name, parameters, and modifiers, while the body contains the logic to be executed. The basic structure of a function is:

solidity

```
function    functionName(parameterType    parameterName)
public returns (returnType) {
    // Function logic
}
```

The visibility modifier, such as public, private, internal or external, determines who can call the function. The return type specifies the value that will be returned by the function.

View, Pure and Payable functions

Solidity categorizes functions based on their impact on the state of the contract. Functions can be marked as view, pure or payable, depending on your behavior.

- **View Functions**
  The functions view they read the status of the contract without changing it. They are used to query state variables and return values.

solidity

```solidity
contract ViewExample {
   uint public storedValue;

   function getValue() public view returns (uint) {
      return storedValue;
   }
}
```

In this case, the function getValue returns the value of the variable storedValue without modifying the contract. Functions view They do not consume gas when called locally, as they do not change the state.

- **Pure Functions**
  The functions pure they do not read or change the status of the contract. They are used to perform calculations and return values based only on the given parameters.

solidity

```solidity
contract PureExample {
    function add(uint a, uint b) public pure returns (uint) {
        return a + b;
    }
}
```

The function add calculates the sum of two numbers without interacting with the contract status. This makes her efficient and independent.

- **Payable Functions**
  The functions payable allow the contract to receive Ether during its execution. They are essential for creating contracts that deal with financial transactions.

solidity

```solidity
contract PayableExample {
    address public owner;

    constructor() {
        owner = msg.sender;
    }

    function deposit() public payable {}

    function withdraw(uint _amount) public {
        require(msg.sender == owner, "Only the owner can withdraw funds");
        require(address(this).balance >= _amount, "Insufficient balance");
        payable(msg.sender).transfer(_amount);
    }
```

}

The function deposit accepts Ether transfers, while withdraw allows the owner to withdraw funds. The keyword payable indicates that a function can receive Ether.

Role Modifiers

Modifiers add conditional logic before or after a function executes. They help reduce redundancy and improve code organization.

solidity

```solidity
contract ModifierExample {
    address public owner;

    modifier onlyOwner() {
        require(msg.sender == owner, "Caller is not the owner");
        _;
    }

    constructor() {
        owner = msg.sender;
    }

    function restrictedAction() public onlyOwner {
        // Logic restricted to the owner
    }
}
```

The modifier onlyOwner checks whether the call was made by the contract owner before executing the main function. Using modifiers improves readability and makes maintenance easier.

Function Overloading

Solidity allows function overloading, which means that multiple functions can have the same name but different parameters. Choosing the correct function is based on the signature of the given parameters.

solidity

```
contract OverloadingExample {
    function add(uint a, uint b) public pure returns (uint) {
        return a + b;
    }

    function add(uint a, uint b, uint c) public pure returns (uint) {
        return a + b + c;
    }
}
```

In the example, two functions add accept different numbers of parameters, allowing flexibility in use.

Return of Values

Functions in Solidity can return single or multiple values. The returned values are defined in the function header.

solidity

```
contract ReturnExample {
    function getSingleValue() public pure returns (uint) {
        return 42;
    }

    function getMultipleValues() public pure returns (uint, string memory) {
        return (42, "Hello, Solidity!");
    }
}
```

The function getSingleValue returns a single value, while getMultipleValues returns a number and a string. The ability to return multiple values is useful for conveying complex information.

Interaction with Other Roles and Contracts

Functions in Solidity can call other internal functions or interact with external contracts. Internal interaction is done directly, while external interaction uses address calls.

solidity

```
contract InternalCallExample {
    function multiply(uint a, uint b) internal pure returns (uint) {
        return a * b;
    }

    function calculate(uint x, uint y) public pure returns (uint) {
        return multiply(x, y);
    }
}

contract ExternalCallExample {
    function getBalance(address _address) public view returns
(uint) {
        return _address.balance;
    }
}
```

In the example, InternalCallExample uses an internal function to perform calculations, while ExternalCallExample interacts with external addresses to check balances.

Recess and Security

Poorly implemented functions can be vulnerable to reentrancy attacks. This type of attack occurs when a function is called repeatedly before its execution is complete, causing unexpected behavior.

solidity

```
contract ReentrancyGuard {
    bool private locked;

    modifier noReentrancy() {
        require(!locked, "Reentrant call detected");
        locked = true;
        _;
        locked = false;
    }

    function secureWithdraw(uint _amount) public
noReentrancy {
        // Withdrawal logic
    }
}
```

The modifier noReentrancy prevents reentrant calls by blocking execution until the current function completes.

Function Optimization

Gas consumption can be reduced by optimizing function logic. Strategies include minimizing complex operations, using loops efficiently, and storing intermediate results.

solidity

```
contract GasOptimization {
    uint[] public numbers;
```

```solidity
function addNumbers(uint[] memory _numbers) public {
    for (uint i = 0; i < _numbers.length; i++) {
        numbers.push(_numbers[i]);
    }
}
}
```

In the example, the function addNumbers uses an efficient loop to add elements to the array numbers.

Testing Functions

Testing is essential to ensure that functions work as expected. Libraries like Hardhat or Truffle make test automation easy.

javascript

```javascript
const { expect } = require("chai");

describe("Function Tests", () => {
  let Contract, contract;

  beforeEach(async () => {
    Contract = await ethers.getContractFactory("ReturnExample");
    contract = await Contract.deploy();
    await contract.deployed();
  });

  it("should return the correct single value", async () => {
    expect(await contract.getSingleValue()).to.equal(42);
  });

  it("should return the correct multiple values", async () => {
    const [num, text] = await contract.getMultipleValues();
    expect(num).to.equal(42);
```

```
    expect(text).to.equal("Hello, Solidity!");
  });
});
```

Automated tests verify return functionality, ensuring contract reliability.

Functions are the core of any contract in Solidity, and their careful implementation is essential for creating effective decentralized applications. Understanding the different types of functions and their applications, combining good security and efficiency practices, is fundamental to taking advantage of the full potential of blockchain development. Once you have mastered these concepts, you can move on to more complex projects with confidence and skill.

CHAPTER 5. FLOW CONTROL AND LOOPS

Flow control is an essential component in programming logic, allowing smart contracts to make decisions based on specific conditions and repeat operations when necessary. In Solidity, the use of structures like if/else, while and for loops make it possible to create more complex and interactive logic, fundamental for various blockchain use cases.

These frameworks are widely employed to manipulate data, validate inputs, manage transactions, and implement algorithms within smart contracts. Adequate implementation of these tools contributes to more efficient, secure and optimized contracts.

Use of if/else

The structure if/else allows execution of different blocks of code based on specific conditions. This structure is especially useful for validations and decisions that affect contract state or behavior.

solidity

```solidity
pragma solidity ^0.8.0;

contract ConditionalExample {
    uint public storedValue;

    function setValue(uint _value) public {
```

```
     if (_value > 100) {
        storedValue = 100; // Maximum limit
     } else if (_value < 10) {
        storedValue = 10; // Minimum limit
     } else {
        storedValue = _value; // Allowed value
     }
  }
}
```

The function setValue adjusts the value of storedValue based on defined conditions. The use of if/else ensures that only values within a specified range are stored. Input validation is an essential practice to prevent unexpected behavior.

Smart contracts often use if/else to manage permissions, such as controlling access to critical functions:

solidity

```
contract AccessControl {
   address private owner;

   constructor() {
      owner = msg.sender;
   }

   function restrictedAction() public view returns (string
memory) {
      if (msg.sender == owner) {
         return "Access granted";
      } else {
         return "Access denied";
      }
   }
}
```

The contract checks whether the person calling the function is the owner and adjusts the response based on that condition. Using this structure adds a layer of security to the contract.

Use of while

O loop while Repeatedly executes a block of code while a condition is true. Although rarely used in Solidity due to gas consumption, it can be useful in specific cases where repetition depends on dynamic conditions.

solidity

```solidity
contract WhileLoopExample {
    uint public sum;

    function calculateSum(uint _limit) public {
        uint i = 0;
        while (i < _limit) {
            sum += i;
            i++;
        }
    }
}
```

The function calculateSum add all numbers smaller than _limit. It is important to limit the number of iterations in loops to avoid running out of gas, which can lead to failed transactions.

THE while can also be used to fetch data or perform operations as long as certain conditions are met:

solidity

```solidity
contract Factorial {
    function computeFactorial(uint _number) public pure
```

```solidity
returns (uint) {
    uint result = 1;
    uint i = _number;
    while (i > 1) {
        result *= i;
        i--;
    }
    return result;
  }
}
```

The function computeFactorial calculates the factorial of a number by repeatedly multiplying until the condition is false. Although simple, algorithms like this demonstrate how loops can be applied to solve mathematical problems.

Use of for

O loop for is more often used in Solidity than the while, as it is more suitable for controlled iterations. It is especially useful for traversing arrays or performing operations in a fixed number of steps.

solidity

```solidity
contract ForLoopExample {
    uint[] public numbers;

    function addNumbers(uint _count) public {
        for (uint i = 0; i < _count; i++) {
            numbers.push(i);
        }
    }
}
```

The function addNumbers adds a series of numbers to the array numbers, using a loop for to control the number of iterations.

Loops for are ideal for handling collections of data in smart contracts.

Efficiency is a critical factor when using loops, especially when iterating over arrays in contracts stored on the blockchain:

solidity

```solidity
contract SumArray {
    function sumElements(uint[] memory _array) public pure
returns (uint) {
        uint total = 0;
        for (uint i = 0; i < _array.length; i++) {
            total += _array[i];
        }
        return total;
    }
}
```

The function sumElements calculates the sum of all elements in a given array. The use of the method length of the array ensures that the loop stops when all elements have been processed.

Comparison between Loops and Optimization

The choice between while and for depends on the scenario. Loops for are preferred when the number of iterations is known, while while It is suitable for dynamic conditions. In both cases, it is essential to minimize complexity to avoid excessive gas costs.

A best practice is to avoid using loops on large data sets. Whenever possible, break operations into smaller steps to improve efficiency. Alternatives such as events or data processed off-chain can be used to reduce the reliance on loops in contracts.

solidity

```
contract OptimizedLoop {
    uint[] public data;

    function batchProcess(uint[] memory _input) public {
        uint length = _input.length;
        for (uint i = 0; i < length; i++) {
            data.push(_input[i]);
        }
    }
}
```

In the example, storing the length of the array in a local variable reduces repeated calls to the method length, saving gas during loop execution.

Flow Control with break and continue

Solidity supports the instructions break and continue, which provide additional control in loops. break immediately ends the loop, while continue skips to the next iteration.

solidity

```
contract BreakContinueExample {
    function findFirstEven(uint[] memory _numbers) public
pure returns (uint) {
        for (uint i = 0; i < _numbers.length; i++) {
            if (_numbers[i] % 2 == 0) {
                return _numbers[i];
            }
        }
        revert("No even numbers found");
    }

    function skipOddNumbers(uint[] memory _numbers) public
pure returns (uint[] memory) {
```

```solidity
    uint[] memory evens = new uint[](_numbers.length);
    uint index = 0;
    for (uint i = 0; i < _numbers.length; i++) {
        if (_numbers[i] % 2 != 0) {
            continue;
        }
        evens[index] = _numbers[i];
        index++;
    }
    return evens;
    }
}
```

The contract contains two functions that demonstrate the use of break and continue. The first returns the first even number in a list, while the second creates a new array containing only even numbers.

Validations and Security in Flow Control

Handling sensitive data in smart contracts requires strict flow control validations. Functions must ensure that invalid inputs are rejected and that loops are optimized to avoid attacks such as excessive gas consumption.

solidity

```solidity
contract SafeControl {
    mapping(address => uint) public balances;

    function deposit() public payable {
        balances[msg.sender] += msg.value;
    }

    function withdraw(uint _amount) public {
        require(balances[msg.sender] >= _amount, "Insufficient
```

```
balance");
      for (uint i = 0; i < 10; i++) {
         // Simulating some logic
      }
      balances[msg.sender] -= _amount;
      payable(msg.sender).transfer(_amount);
   }
}
```

The contract demonstrates the combination of validations and loops in a real scenario. The use of require ensures that conditions are met before executing the loop.

Integration with Advanced Frameworks

Combining loops with other Solidity structures, such as mappings and events, expands their applicability to more complex smart contracts.

solidity

```
contract AdvancedUsage {
    mapping(address => uint) public balances;
    event Transfer(address indexed from, address indexed to,
uint amount);

    function distributeRewards(address[] memory _recipients,
uint _amount) public {
        uint totalCost = _recipients.length * _amount;
        require(balances[msg.sender] >= totalCost, "Insufficient
balance");

        for (uint i = 0; i < _recipients.length; i++) {
            balances[msg.sender] -= _amount;
            balances[_recipients[i]] += _amount;
            emit Transfer(msg.sender, _recipients[i], _amount);
```

```
        }
    }
}
```

The function distributeRewards Distributes rewards to a list of addresses and records transfers as events. This approach combines validation, loops, and interaction with the contract state.

Applications and Good Practices

Flow control and loops in Solidity are fundamental to implementing logic that depends on conditions and repetitions. Its correct use improves the functionality and security of smart contracts, enabling complex interactions efficiently.

Developers should always consider the impact of loops on gas consumption, using optimizations and alternatives whenever possible. Adopting good practices, such as rigorous validations and limits on iterations, is essential to building secure and effective contracts. Mastering these tools empowers developers to solve challenging problems and create innovative solutions in the blockchain ecosystem.

CHAPTER 6. EVENTS AND LOGS

Events play a key role in the development of smart contracts in Solidity, enabling communication between contracts and external applications that interact with the blockchain. By logging on the blockchain, events provide an efficient and reliable way to monitor changes to the state of contracts. These records are widely used to track transactions, record critical information, and provide real-time feedback on operations performed by contracts.

What are Events in Solidity?

Events in Solidity are statements that write data to blockchain logs. These logs are not part of the permanent storage of the contract, but are stored in a special structure that can be accessed by decentralized applications (dApps) and external tools such as JavaScript libraries that use Web3.js or Ethers.js. Events allow smart contracts to issue notifications to let external applications know when a specific action has occurred.

The definition of an event in Solidity uses the keyword event, followed by a name and parameters that define the data to be recorded:

solidity

```
pragma solidity ^0.8.0;

contract EventLogger {
    event ValueChanged(address indexed sender, uint oldValue,
uint newValue);
```

```
uint public value;

function updateValue(uint _newValue) public {
    uint oldValue = value;
    value = _newValue;
    emit ValueChanged(msg.sender, oldValue, _newValue);
  }
}
```

In the contract, the event ValueChanged is declared to record information about changes to the variable value. The modifier indexed in sender allows future queries to be performed based on this parameter, making the record more accessible to external applications.

How Events Work on Blockchain?

When an event is emitted, its data is stored in the corresponding transaction logs. These logs do not affect contract status and do not consume significant gas, making them an efficient solution for recording information. A log consists of three main parts:

1. **Topic Subscription**: A unique identification based on the event hash.
2. **Indexed Topics**: Fields marked as indexed, allowing quick queries.
3. **Unindexed Data**: Additional information provided by the event.

Logs can be accessed by external tools using the topic subscription and indexed parameters to filter relevant events.

Emitting Events in Smart Contracts

Event issuance is done with the instruction emit, followed by the name of the event and the data to be recorded. This practice is common in functions that change the contract state or perform important actions.

solidity

```
pragma solidity ^0.8.0;

contract PaymentProcessor {
    event PaymentReceived(address indexed payer, uint amount);

    function pay() public payable {
        require(msg.value > 0, "Payment must be greater than zero");
        emit PaymentReceived(msg.sender, msg.value);
    }
}
```

In the contract, the event PaymentReceived is issued whenever the function pay is called, recording the payer's address and the amount sent. This record can be used by applications to monitor payments in real time.

Tracking Data with Events

Events are often used to track token transfers, ownership changes, and other critical activities in smart contracts. A common example is the use of events in token contracts that follow standards like ERC-20:

solidity

```
pragma solidity ^0.8.0;

contract Token {
    string public name = "Sample Token";
```

```solidity
string public symbol = "STK";
uint8 public decimals = 18;
uint public totalSupply;

mapping(address => uint) public balanceOf;

event Transfer(address indexed from, address indexed to,
uint value);

constructor(uint _initialSupply) {
    totalSupply = _initialSupply;
    balanceOf[msg.sender] = _initialSupply;
    emit Transfer(address(0), msg.sender, _initialSupply);
}

function transfer(address _to, uint _value) public returns
(bool success) {
    require(balanceOf[msg.sender] >= _value, "Insufficient
balance");
    balanceOf[msg.sender] -= _value;
    balanceOf[_to] += _value;
    emit Transfer(msg.sender, _to, _value);
    return true;
}
}
```

The event Transfer is used to record all token transfers. This allows wallets and blockchain explorers to track token movements without needing to interact directly with the contract.

Querying Events with External Tools

The recorded events can be queried by decentralized applications to provide information to users. Libraries like Web3.js and Ethers.js offer methods for fetching and monitoring events in real time.

With Web3.js, you can configure a listener to capture events from a contract:

javascript

```javascript
const Web3 = require('web3');
const web3 = new Web3('https://mainnet.infura.io/v3/
YOUR_INFURA_PROJECT_ID');

const contractABI = [ /* ABI given to the contract */ ];
const contractAddress = '0x123...'; // Contract address
const contract = new web3.eth.Contract(contractABI,
contractAddress);

contract.events.Transfer({
    filter: { from: '0x456...' }, // Filtro opcional
    fromBlock: 0
}, (error, event) => {
    if (!error) {
        console.log(event.returnValues);
    }
});
```

This code monitors events Transfer issued by the contract, filtering by a specific address. Applications can use this data to update user interfaces or perform automated actions.

Good Practices in Using Events

Events are a powerful tool, but their use must follow best practices to ensure efficiency and clarity:

- **Avoid Unnecessary Data**: Store only essential information to reduce log size and associated costs.

- **Limit Indexed Topics**: The number of indexed fields should be minimized to optimize queries.
- **Emit Consistent Events**: Following well-established standards, such as those defined by ERC standards, facilitates integration with tools and dApps.

Practical Event Applications

Events are widely used in various scenarios, such as:

1. **Transaction Monitoring**
   Records of payments, transfers, and status changes help apps provide real-time feedback to users.
2. **Audit and Transparency**
   Events make contract operations more auditable, recording information for future reference.
3. **Triggers for Automation**
   Applications can use events as triggers to automatically perform actions, such as sending notifications or starting off-chain processes.

solidity

```solidity
pragma solidity ^0.8.0;

contract Auction {
    address public highestBidder;
    uint public highestBid;

    event NewHighestBid(address indexed bidder, uint amount);

    function placeBid() public payable {
        require(msg.value > highestBid, "Bid must be higher than current highest bid");
        highestBidder = msg.sender;
        highestBid = msg.value;
        emit NewHighestBid(msg.sender, msg.value);
```

```
    }
}
```

In the auction contract, the event NewHighestBid is issued whenever a higher offer is made. This registration allows auction participants to track bids in real time.

Challenges and Limitations

Although events are an efficient tool, they have some limitations:

- **Off-chain Access**: Events cannot be read directly by other contracts, being accessible only by external tools.
- **Gas Cost**: Although events are cheaper than storing data in state variables, they still incur costs.
- **Indexing Limitation**: Only three parameters can be indexed in an event, limiting the efficiency of complex queries.

These limitations must be considered when designing smart contracts to ensure that events are used effectively.

Events in Solidity are essential for building efficient, interactive smart contracts. They connect contracts with the outside world, enabling transaction tracking and communication with decentralized applications. Understanding how to issue, record and query events allows developers to create contracts that are more functional and aligned with the needs of the blockchain ecosystem.

By following best practices and using events strategically, it is possible to create robust solutions that take advantage of the full potential of smart contract technology, offering greater transparency, automation and efficiency in decentralized applications.

CHAPTER 7. ARRAYS AND MAPPINGS

Arrays and mappings are fundamental data structures in Solidity that allow you to store, organize and access information efficiently in smart contracts. Arrays provide a linear structure for grouping elements of the same type, while mappings create key-value associations, ideal for representing complex relationships and indexed data.

Understanding and applying these frameworks is essential for building smart contracts that require dynamic management of information such as user records, account balances, or transaction lists.

Arrays em Solidity

Arrays in Solidity store elements of the same type in a sequential manner. They can be fixed or dynamic in size, depending on the needs of the contract. Dynamic arrays can grow or shrink during execution, making them more versatile for situations where the number of elements is not known in advance.

Fixed Size Arrays

Fixed-size arrays have a defined number of elements and cannot be changed after creation.

solidity

```solidity
pragma solidity ^0.8.0;

contract FixedArray {
    uint[5] public numbers = [1, 2, 3, 4, 5];

    function getElement(uint index) public view returns (uint) {
        return numbers[index];
    }

    function setElement(uint index, uint value) public {
        numbers[index] = value;
    }
}
```

In the example, the array numbers stores five integers. The function getElement returns the value at the specified index, while setElement allows you to change the value in an index.

Dynamic Arrays

Dynamic arrays have no predefined element limit and can grow as needed.

solidity

```solidity
pragma solidity ^0.8.0;

contract DynamicArray {
    uint[] public numbers;

    function addNumber(uint value) public {
        numbers.push(value);
    }

    function getNumbers() public view returns (uint[] memory) {
        return numbers;
    }
}
```

```solidity
function getLength() public view returns (uint) {
    return numbers.length;
  }
}
```

The contract uses the method push to add elements to dynamic array numbers. The function getNumbers returns the entire array, while getLength gives the current number of elements.

Removing Elements in Dynamic Arrays

Removing elements from dynamic arrays can be challenging because Solidity does not automatically adjust indexes. To maintain data integrity, developers must implement custom logic.

solidity

```solidity
pragma solidity ^0.8.0;

contract ArrayRemoval {
    uint[] public numbers;

    function addNumber(uint value) public {
        numbers.push(value);
    }

    function removeNumber(uint index) public {
        require(index < numbers.length, "Index out of bounds");
        numbers[index] = numbers[numbers.length - 1];
        numbers.pop();
    }
}
```

The method removeNumber replaces the value at the specified index with the last element of the array and then reduces the size of the array with pop. This approach is efficient, but it changes the order of the elements.

Mappings in Solidity

Mappings are data structures that associate keys with values, offering fast and efficient access. Unlike arrays, mappings do not store keys or values in a specific order, making them ideal for storing direct relationships.

Declaration of Mappings

Mappings in Solidity are defined with key type and value type. The key must be of a simple type, such as address or uint, while the value can be any valid type.

solidity

```solidity
pragma solidity ^0.8.0;

contract SimpleMapping {
    mapping(address => uint) public balances;

    function setBalance(uint value) public {
        balances[msg.sender] = value;
    }

    function getBalance(address account) public view returns
(uint) {
        return balances[account];
    }
}
```

In the example, the mapping balances associates addresses with integer values, representing a basic balance management system. The function setBalance defines the balance of the caller, and getBalance returns the balance of a specific address.

Mappings with Structures

Mappings can store structures as values, allowing complex information to be organized efficiently.

solidity

```solidity
pragma solidity ^0.8.0;

contract MappingWithStruct {
    struct User {
        string name;
        uint age;
    }

    mapping(address => User) public users;

    function registerUser(string memory name, uint age) public
{
        users[msg.sender] = User(name, age);
    }

    function getUser(address userAddress) public view returns
(string memory, uint) {
        User memory user = users[userAddress];
        return (user.name, user.age);
    }
}
```

The contract uses the mapping users to associate addresses with user data, including name and age. The structure User organizes the data clearly, and the functions allow you to record and access the information.

Nested Mappings

Mappings can also be nested, creating more complex associations.

solidity

```solidity
pragma solidity ^0.8.0;

contract NestedMapping {
    mapping(address => mapping(uint => bool)) public
userPermissions;

    function setPermission(uint permission, bool status) public {
        userPermissions[msg.sender][permission] = status;
    }

    function hasPermission(address user, uint permission)
public view returns (bool) {
        return userPermissions[user][permission];
    }
}
```

The nested mapping userPermissions stores specific permissions for each user. The function setPermission adjusts the status of a permission, while hasPermission checks whether a user has a specific permission.

Comparison between Arrays and Mappings

Arrays and mappings have distinct characteristics that make them suitable for different use cases:

- Arrays are useful when the order of elements is important or when it is necessary to iterate over all elements.
- Mappings are ideal for quick searches and storing key-value relationships, but they do not allow direct iteration.

Developers must choose the most appropriate framework based

on the requirements of their smart contract.

Good Practices in Using Arrays and Mappings

- **Input Validation**: Ensure indexes and keys are valid before accessing arrays or mappings.
- **Loop Optimization**: Minimize the use of loops in large arrays to reduce gas costs.
- **Efficient Use of Mappings**: Avoid storing unnecessary data, as mappings are optimized for direct access.

Array and Mapping Integration

Combining arrays and mappings allows you to create more flexible and powerful data structures.

solidity

```solidity
pragma solidity ^0.8.0;

contract ArrayMappingIntegration {
    mapping(address => uint[]) public userTransactions;

    function addTransaction(uint amount) public {
        userTransactions[msg.sender].push(amount);
    }

    function getTransactions(address user) public view returns
(uint[] memory) {
        return userTransactions[user];
    }
}
```

The contract records user transactions using an array mapping. Combining the structures makes it easier to track multiple entries related to each user.

Arrays and mappings are indispensable tools in Solidity, providing flexibility and efficiency in data management in smart contracts. Mastering these frameworks allows developers to create robust, secure and scalable decentralized applications, catering to a wide range of scenarios in the blockchain ecosystem.

CHAPTER 8. STRUCTURES AND ENUMS

Structures and enums are powerful and versatile components in Solidity, allowing developers to organize data and represent states clearly and efficiently. These features provide a way to create custom types and manage more complex information in smart contracts. Structures are used to group related data into a single entity, while enums provide an efficient way of dealing with pre-defined and fixed states.

The ability to model complex data and accurately represent specific states is essential for building robust and scalable smart contracts. Structures and enums play an important role in diverse applications in the blockchain ecosystem, from voting systems to financial market contracts.

Structures in Solidity

Structures allow you to group multiple types of data into a single entity. This facilitates the management of related information and improves the readability and organization of the contract.

Creating and Using Structures

To create a structure, the keyword struct, followed by the name and fields that make up the structure.

solidity

```
pragma solidity ^0.8.0;

contract StructExample {
```

```solidity
struct User {
    string name;
    uint age;
    address wallet;
}

User public admin;

function setAdmin(string memory _name, uint _age, address _wallet) public {
    admin = User(_name, _age, _wallet);
}

function getAdmin() public view returns (string memory, uint, address) {
    return (admin.name, admin.age, admin.wallet);
}
}
```

The contract defines the structure User, which groups information such as name, age and wallet address. The function setAdmin configures the structure values, while getAdmin returns the stored data.

Using Structures in Arrays and Mappings

Structures can be used in arrays and mappings to manage complex data sets.

solidity

```solidity
contract StructArray {
    struct Product {
        string name;
        uint price;
        uint stock;
    }
```

```solidity
    Product[] public products;

    function addProduct(string memory _name, uint _price, uint
_stock) public {
        products.push(Product(_name, _price, _stock));
    }

    function getProduct(uint index) public view returns (string
memory, uint, uint) {
        Product memory product = products[index];
        return (product.name, product.price, product.stock);
    }
}
```

The contract uses an array of structures Product to store information about products. The function addProduct adds a new item to the array, while getProduct retrieves information for a product based on the index.

With mappings, structures can be associated with specific keys, such as addresses.

solidity

```solidity
contract StructMapping {
    struct Account {
        string owner;
        uint balance;
    }

    mapping(address => Account) public accounts;

    function createAccount(string memory _owner) public {
        accounts[msg.sender] = Account(_owner, 0);
    }

    function deposit() public payable {
```

```
    accounts[msg.sender].balance += msg.value;
  }

  function getBalance(address _account) public view returns
(uint) {
    return accounts[_account].balance;
  }
}
```

The contract associates the structure Account to addresses, allowing you to manage information about user accounts, including the balance and owner name.

Updating Fields in Structures

Structure fields can be updated individually or in combination.

solidity

```
contract StructUpdate {
  struct Task {
    string description;
    bool completed;
  }

  Task public task;

  function setTask(string memory _description) public {
    task = Task(_description, false);
  }

  function completeTask() public {
    task.completed = true;
  }
}
```

The contract initializes the task with a description and status. false. The function completeTask prepare the other state true, indicating that the task has been completed.

Enums em Solidity

Enums, or enumerators, allow you to define a set of fixed states or options that a contract can take. They are useful for representing finite states, such as steps in a process or specific conditions.

Declaration and Usage of Enums

To declare an enum, you use the keyword enum, followed by the name and possible values.

solidity

```solidity
contract EnumExample {
    enum status
        Pending,
        Shipped,
        Delivered,
        Cancelled
    }

    Status public currentStatus;

    function setStatus(Status _status) public {
        currentStatus = _status;
    }

    function getStatus() public view returns (Status) {
        return currentStatus;
    }
}
```

The contract defines the enum Status with four possible states.

The function setStatus allows you to set the current state, while getStatus returns the current state.

Enum Manipulation

Enums can be manipulated based on explicit indices or values.

solidity

```solidity
contract EnumManipulation {
    enum Level {
        Low,
        Medium,
        High
    }

    Level public securityLevel;

    function increaseSecurity() public {
        if (securityLevel == Level.Low) {
            securityLevel = Level.Medium;
        } else if (securityLevel == Level.Medium) {
            securityLevel = Level.High;
        }
    }

    function resetSecurity() public {
        securityLevel = Level.Low;
    }
}
```

The contract adjusts the security level based on the current state. The function increaseSecurity promotes the level of security, while resetSecurity resets to the lowest level.

Using Enums in Structures

Enums can be combined with structures to model complex data with defined states.

solidity

```solidity
contract StructEnum {
    enum OrderStatus {
        Pending,
        Shipped,
        Delivered
    }

    struct Order {
        uint id;
        string product;
        OrderStatus status;
    }

    mapping(uint => Order) public orders;

    function createOrder(uint _id, string memory _product) public {
        orders[_id] = Order(_id, _product, OrderStatus.Pending);
    }

    function updateStatus(uint _id, OrderStatus _status) public {
        orders[_id].status = _status;
    }

    function getOrderStatus(uint _id) public view returns (OrderStatus) {
        return orders[_id].status;
    }
}
```

The contract combines the structure Order with the enum OrderStatus to manage orders and their status. The function updateStatus allows you to change the status of an order, while getOrderStatus returns the current state.

Good Practices in Using Structures and Enums

- **Clarity and Organization**: Name structures and enums in a descriptive way to make the code easier to understand.
- **Limited States**: Use enums only for fixed and finite states, avoiding excessive values.
- **Avoid Cyclical Dependencies**: Ensure that structs and enums do not create complex or confusing dependencies on each other.

Integration of Structures and Enums

Combining frameworks and enums allows you to create robust and flexible smart contracts.

solidity

```
contract ComplexModel {
    enum Role {
        Admin,
        User,
        Guest
    }

    struct Profile {
        string name;
        Role role;
    }

    mapping(address => Profile) public profiles;

    function register(string memory _name, Role _role) public {
        profiles[msg.sender] = Profile(_name, _role);
    }
```

```solidity
    function getProfile(address _address) public view returns
(string memory, Role) {
        Profile memory profile = profiles[_address];
        return (profile.name, profile.role);
    }
}
```

The contract manages user profiles with different roles using a combination of enums and structures. The integration of both tools results in a clear and scalable solution.

Structures and enums are indispensable elements in Solidity for modeling complex data and managing states efficiently. Creating custom types not only improves contract readability and organization, but also allows developers to accurately represent real-world scenarios in smart contracts. Mastery of these tools is essential to build robust, scalable decentralized applications aligned with the best practices of the blockchain ecosystem.

CHAPTER 9. MODIFIERS AND INHERITANCE

Modifiers and inheritance are fundamental elements of Solidity, designed to facilitate code reuse and ensure the security and organization of smart contracts. Modifiers allow you to add conditional logic to functions, while inheritance allows you to create base contracts that can be extended by others, promoting modularity and efficiency in contract development.

These tools are widely used in large-scale projects such as decentralized finance (DeFi) platforms, blockchain-based games, and Decentralized Autonomous Organizations (DAOs). A deep understanding of modifiers and inheritance is essential for writing secure, organized, and maintainable smart contracts.

Custom Modifiers

Modifiers in Solidity are blocks of code that add conditional logic to functions. They are used to validate conditions before executing a function or to perform pre-defined actions in conjunction with the function logic.

Modifier Creation

Modifiers are declared with the keyword modifier, followed by a name and the code that defines the conditional logic. The symbol _ indicates where execution of the main function will resume.

solidity

```solidity
pragma solidity ^0.8.0;

contract ModifierExample {
   address private owner;

   modifier onlyOwner() {
      require(msg.sender == owner, "Caller is not the owner");
      _;
   }

   constructor() {
      owner = msg.sender;
   }

   function changeOwner(address newOwner) public
onlyOwner {
      owner = newOwner;
   }
}
```

The modifier onlyOwner checks whether the function caller is the owner of the contract before executing the main logic. The function changeOwner uses this modifier to restrict access.

Modifiers with Arguments

Modifiers can accept arguments, allowing dynamic validations.

solidity

```solidity
contract ModifierWithArgs {
   uint public minimumAmount = 10;

   modifier greaterThan(uint value) {
      require(value > minimumAmount, "Value is too low");
      _;
   }
```

```solidity
function setMinimum(uint newMinimum) public {
    minimumAmount = newMinimum;
}

function deposit(uint amount) public greaterThan(amount)
{
    // Logic for deposit
}
}
```

The modifier greaterThan checks if the given value is greater than a minimum threshold before allowing the function to execute deposit.

Using Modifiers for Security

Modifiers are often used to implement security measures such as indentation protection.

solidity

```
contract ReentrancyGuard {
    bool private locked;

    modifier noReentrancy() {
        require(!locked, "Reentrant call detected");
        locked = true;
        _;
        locked = false;
    }

    function withdraw(uint amount) public noReentrancy {
        // Logic for withdrawal
    }
}
```

The modifier noReentrancy prevents the function from being

called again before completion, protecting the contract against reentrancy attacks.

Inheritance in Solidity

Inheritance in Solidity allows contracts to share functionality, promoting code reuse and reducing redundancies. A contract can inherit from another using the keyword is.

Declaration of Inheritance

To create a contract that inherits another, simply add the keyword is followed by the name of the base contract.

solidity

```solidity
pragma solidity ^0.8.0;

contract BaseContract {
    string public baseMessage = "This is the base contract";

    function baseFunction() public view returns (string memory) {
        return baseMessage;
    }
}

contract DerivedContract is BaseContract {
    function getBaseMessage() public view returns (string memory) {
        return baseFunction();
    }
}
```

The contract DerivedContract inherits from BaseContract, allowing access to the function and public variables of the base contract.

Multiple Inheritance

Solidity supports multiple inheritance, allowing a contract to inherit from multiple base contracts.

solidity

```
contract A {
    string public messageA = "Contract A";

    function getMessageA() public view returns (string memory)
{
        return messageA;
    }
}

contract B {
    string public messageB = "Contract B";

    function getMessageB() public view returns (string memory)
{
        return messageB;
    }
}

contract C is A, B {
    function getCombinedMessages() public view returns (string
memory) {
        return   string(abi.encodePacked(getMessageA(),  " & ",
getMessageB()));
    }
}
```

The contract C herd of A and B, combining functionalities of both. The function getCombinedMessages returns messages from both base contracts.

Handling Conflicts in Inheritance

When base contracts have functions or variables with the same name, Solidity requires the developer to explicitly resolve the conflicts.

solidity

```
contract Parent1 {
    function greet() public pure virtual returns (string memory)
{
        return "Hello from Parent1";
    }
}

contract Parent2 {
    function greet() public pure virtual returns (string memory)
{
        return "Hello from Parent2";
    }
}

contract Child is Parent1, Parent2 {
    function greet() public pure override(Parent1, Parent2)
returns (string memory) {
        return string(abi.encodePacked(Parent1.greet(), " and ",
Parent2.greet()));
    }
}
```

The contract Child resolves conflict between functions greet inherited from Parent1 and Parent2 implementing your own version of the function.

Use of Abstract Contracts

Abstract contracts define structures that must be implemented by derived contracts. They are useful for creating standardized interfaces.

solidity

```solidity
abstract contract AbstractContract {
    function abstractFunction() public virtual returns (string memory);
}

contract ConcreteContract is AbstractContract {
    function abstractFunction() public pure override returns (string memory) {
        return "Concrete implementation";
    }
}
```

The contract AbstractContract defines an abstract function that must be implemented by any contract that inherits it. The contract ConcreteContract provides the implementation of the function.

Modifier Combination and Inheritance

Modifiers and inheritance can be combined to create reusable and secure contracts.

solidity

```solidity
contract BaseAccessControl {
    address private owner;

    modifier onlyOwner() {
        require(msg.sender == owner, "Not the owner");
        _;
    }
```

```
constructor() {
    owner = msg.sender;
}
}

contract ExtendedContract is BaseAccessControl {
    function sensitiveOperation() public onlyOwner {
        // Logic restricted to owner
    }
}
```

The contract BaseAccessControl defines property logic and modifier onlyOwner. The contract ExtendedContract inherits this functionality and uses it to protect a sensitive function.

Good Practices in Using Modifiers and Inheritance

- **Modularity**: Use modifiers and inheritance to separate logic and responsibilities.
- **Security**: Implement modifiers to validate conditions and protect against attacks.
- **Readability**: Maintain clear and well-structured contracts to facilitate maintenance.
- **Avoid Excessive Multiple Inheritance**: Reduce contract complexity by minimizing the use of multiple inheritance.

Modifiers and inheritance are indispensable tools in developing smart contracts in Solidity, offering efficient ways to reuse code, implement conditional logic, and protect functions. The combination of these features empowers developers to create more robust, secure and scalable contracts, enabling the construction of innovative solutions in the blockchain ecosystem. By adopting best practices, it is possible to maximize the efficiency and security of contracts, promoting a more efficient development experience aligned with market demands.

CHAPTER 10. PAYMENTS AND TRANSFERS

The manipulation of Ether in smart contracts is an essential functionality in Solidity, enabling the creation of decentralized financial applications, automated payment systems and contracts that manage digital assets. To perform Ether transfers between contracts or addresses, Solidity offers three main methods: send, transfer and call. Each of them has specific characteristics, advantages and risks that need to be understood to guarantee the security and efficiency of the contract.

This chapter explores how to manage payments in smart contracts, discusses the differences between transfer methods, and provides guidance on best practices to avoid issues such as reentrancy attacks.

Basic Ether Manipulation in Contracts

A smart contract can programmatically receive and send Ether. The special function receive allows contracts to accept Ether directly, while the function fallback serves as a backup mechanism for calls that do not match any defined function.

Receiving Ether

For a contract to accept Ether, it must include the keyword payable in the relevant functions. The function receive is used to accept simple payments:

solidity

```
pragma solidity ^0.8.0;
```

```solidity
contract EtherReceiver {
   event EtherReceived(address indexed sender, uint amount);

   receive() external payable {
      emit EtherReceived(msg.sender, msg.value);
   }

   function getBalance() public view returns (uint) {
      return address(this).balance;
   }
}
```

The function receive records the sender's address and the amount sent in an event, while getBalance returns the total balance stored in the contract.

Transferring Ether

A contract can send Ether to another address using the methods send, transfer or call. The choice of method depends on factors such as security and compatibility.

Difference between send, transfer and call

The three available methods for transferring Ether have significant differences in terms of behavior, security, and recommended use.

Method transfer

The method transfer is simple and secure, transferring a fixed amount of Ether to the specified address. It automatically rolls back the transaction in case of failure.

solidity

```solidity
contract EtherTransfer {
```

```
    function sendEther(address payable recipient) public payable
{
        recipient.transfer(msg.value);
    }
}
```

The method transfer provides basic protection against reentrant attacks by limiting the gas available for performing fallback functions on the recipient to 2300 units. However, this limitation can be a problem in cases where the recipient needs more gas to complete its operations.

Method send

The method send is similar to transfer, but returns a boolean value indicating the success or failure of the transaction, rather than automatically rolling back on error. It also limits the available gas to 2300 units.

solidity

```
contract EtherSend {
    function sendEther(address payable recipient) public payable
{
        bool success = recipient.send(msg.value);
        require(success, "Transfer failed");
    }
}
```

Although the send allows you to manually handle failures, it is less secure than transfer, as it depends on the proper implementation of error handling in the contract.

Method call

The method call it is the most flexible and powerful, but also the most dangerous. It allows you to specify the amount of Ether to be transferred and the gas available to execute the call. However, it does not automatically roll back on failure, requiring explicit rollback handling.

solidity

```
contract EtherCall {
    function sendEther(address payable recipient) public payable
{

        (bool success, ) = recipient.call{value: msg.value}("");
        require(success, "Transfer failed");
    }
}
```

THE call It is widely used due to its flexibility, but requires additional care to avoid vulnerabilities such as reentrancy attacks.

Dealing with Reentrant Attacks

Reentrancy attacks occur when a malicious contract exploits callback functions to execute repeated calls before the initial execution is complete. This type of attack can lead to the depletion of funds in vulnerable contracts.

Preventing reentrancy attacks involves using secure standards and best practices, such as updating the contract state before transferring funds.

solidity

```
contract ReentrancySafe {
    mapping(address => uint) private balances;

    function deposit() public payable {
        balances[msg.sender] += msg.value;
```

```
    }

function withdraw(uint amount) public {
    require(balances[msg.sender] >= amount, "Insufficient
balance");

    balances[msg.sender] -= amount;

    (bool success, ) = msg.sender.call{value: amount}("");
    require(success, "Withdrawal failed");
    }
}
```

In this example, the user's balance is updated before the Ether transfer, protecting the contract against reentrancy attacks.

Using Events for Monitoring

Events are an efficient way to record Ether transfers and provide real-time feedback to applications that interact with the contract.

solidity

```
contract EtherLogger {
    event EtherSent(address indexed from, address indexed to,
uint amount);

    function transferEther(address payable recipient) public
payable {
        recipient.transfer(msg.value);
        emit EtherSent(msg.sender, recipient, msg.value);
    }
}
```

The event EtherSent records the sender, recipient and amount transferred, facilitating transaction tracking.

Fund Management in Complex Contracts

Contracts that deal with multiple users or financial applications require efficient management of funds. Mapping user balances and implementing robust deposit and withdrawal functions are common practices.

solidity

```solidity
contract SharedWallet {
    mapping(address => uint) public balances;

    function deposit() public payable {
        balances[msg.sender] += msg.value;
    }

    function withdraw(uint amount) public {
        require(balances[msg.sender] >= amount, "Insufficient balance");
        balances[msg.sender] -= amount;

        (bool success, ) = msg.sender.call{value: amount}("");
        require(success, "Withdrawal failed");
    }

    function getBalance() public view returns (uint) {
        return balances[msg.sender];
    }
}
```

In this contract, each user has an individual balance, allowing safe deposits and withdrawals. The use of call ensures flexibility, while validations protect funds.

Good Practices in Ether Handling

- **Strict Validations**: Check entries such as transaction amounts and balances to avoid invalid transfers.
- **Indentation Prevention**: Update contract status before transferring Ether.
- **Monitoring Events**: Emit events to record transfers and facilitate audits.
- **Cautious use of** call: Use call only when necessary, ensuring that error handling is implemented correctly.

Manipulating Ether in smart contracts is an essential skill for developing robust and secure decentralized applications. Understand the differences between send, transfer and call, as well as security best practices, empowers developers to create solutions that maximize efficiency and protection against attacks. Responsible use of these tools, combined with secure development practices, ensures the integrity and performance of contracts in the blockchain ecosystem.

CHAPTER 11. SECURITY IN SMART CONTRACTS

Security is a critical concern in the development of smart contracts. As contracts are immutable once they are deployed on the blockchain, any vulnerability could lead to irreparable financial losses and reputational damage. Ensuring protection against attacks and implementing good secure coding practices are fundamental steps to building reliable and resilient smart contracts.

This chapter covers the main types of vulnerabilities, such as backflow and spillover, and presents practices to avoid common mistakes, as well as advanced strategies to mitigate risks and improve the robustness of contracts.

Protection against Common Vulnerabilities

Recess

Reentrancy is one of the most exploited vulnerabilities in smart contracts. The attack occurs when an external contract calls back the function of the vulnerable contract before the original execution is completed, taking advantage of non-updated balances or states.

Recess Attack Scenario

Consider a simple fund management contract:

solidity

```solidity
pragma solidity ^0.8.0;

contract VulnerableContract {
    mapping(address => uint) public balances;

    function deposit() public payable {
        balances[msg.sender] += msg.value;
    }

    function withdraw(uint amount) public {
        require(balances[msg.sender] >= amount, "Insufficient
balance");
        (bool success, ) = msg.sender.call{value: amount}("");
        require(success, "Transfer failed");
        balances[msg.sender] -= amount;
    }
}
```

This contract is vulnerable to reentrancy attacks because the user's balance state (balances[msg.sender]) is updated after the transfer of Ether, allowing a malicious contract to call the function withdraw repeatedly before updating.

Mitigating Indentation

An effective strategy to avoid reentrancy is to update the contract state before transferring Ether or calling external contracts.

solidity

```solidity
contract ReentrancySafe {
    mapping(address => uint) public balances;

    function deposit() public payable {
```

```solidity
        balances[msg.sender] += msg.value;
    }

    function withdraw(uint amount) public {
        require(balances[msg.sender] >= amount, "Insufficient
balance");
        balances[msg.sender] -= amount;
        (bool success, ) = msg.sender.call{value: amount}("");
        require(success, "Transfer failed");
    }
}
```

Updating the user's balance before the transfer prevents subsequent calls from exploiting inconsistent states.

Another method is to use an execution lock to prevent multiple simultaneous inputs to the same function.

solidity

```solidity
contract ReentrancyGuard {
    bool private locked;

    modifier noReentrancy() {
        require(!locked, "Reentrant call detected");
        locked = true;
        _;
        locked = false;
    }

    function withdraw(uint amount) public noReentrancy {
        // Logic for withdrawal
    }
}
```

The modifier noReentrancy guarantees that the function is executed only once per call.

Overflow e Underflow

Overflow and underflow occur when arithmetic operations exceed the maximum or minimum limits of a data type, resulting in unexpected values. In modern versions of Solidity (starting from 0.8.0), these operations are automatically checked, rolling back the transaction in case of error.

Managing Secure Arithmetic

Although modern versions of Solidity provide native protection, you can use the library SafeMath on legacy projects to ensure secure operations.

solidity

```solidity
pragma solidity ^0.8.0;

library SafeMath {
    function add(uint a, uint b) internal pure returns (uint) {
        uint c = a + b;
        require(c >= a, "Addition overflow");
        return c;
    }

    function sub(uint a, uint b) internal pure returns (uint) {
        require(b <= a, "Subtraction underflow");
        uint c = a - b;
        return c;
    }
}
```

Developers can integrate these functions into their contracts to validate arithmetic operations.

solidity

```
contract SafeArithmetic {
    using SafeMath for uint;

    uint public totalSupply;

    function mint(uint amount) public {
        totalSupply = totalSupply.add(amount);
    }
}
```

Phishing Attacks and Name Conflicts

Phishing attacks exploit confusion in contract or role names. To mitigate these risks, use clear identifiers and document code in detail. Additionally, adopting the EIP-165 standard allows contracts to declare support for specific interfaces, avoiding ambiguities.

Good Secure Coding Practices

Strict Validations

Always validate inputs to avoid unexpected values that could compromise the contract logic.

solidity

```
contract InputValidation {
    function transfer(address recipient, uint amount) public {
        require(recipient != address(0), "Invalid address");
        require(amount > 0, "Amount must be greater than zero");
        // Logic for transfer
    }
}
```

Limited Use of call

Although call be flexible, it is more prone to errors. Prefer transfer or send for simple Ether transfers and use call only when necessary, implementing error handling.

solidity

```solidity
contract SafeCall {
    function sendEther(address payable recipient) public payable {

        (bool success, ) = recipient.call{value: msg.value}("");
        require(success, "Transfer failed");
    }
}
```

Modularity Maintenance

Separate logic into smaller contracts or functions for easier auditing and improved reusability.

solidity

```solidity
contract ModularContract {
    function validateTransfer(address recipient, uint amount) internal pure {
        require(recipient != address(0), "Invalid address");
        require(amount > 0, "Amount must be greater than zero");
    }

    function executeTransfer(address payable recipient, uint amount) internal {
        (bool success, ) = recipient.call{value: amount}("");
        require(success, "Transfer failed");
    }

    function transfer(address payable recipient, uint amount) public payable {
        validateTransfer(recipient, amount);
        executeTransfer(recipient, amount);
```

```
    }
}
```

Using Events for Auditing

Emitting events to record important actions facilitates audits and contract monitoring.

solidity

```
contract AuditTrail {
    event TransferMade(address indexed from, address indexed
to, uint amount);

    function transfer(address payable recipient, uint amount)
public payable {
        (bool success, ) = recipient.call{value: amount}("");
        require(success, "Transfer failed");
        emit TransferMade(msg.sender, recipient, amount);
    }
}
```

Access Control Implementation

Protect sensitive functions by implementing role-based access control.

solidity

```
contract RoleBasedAccess {
    address private owner;

    modifier onlyOwner() {
        require(msg.sender == owner, "Access denied");
        _;
    }

    constructor() {
        owner = msg.sender;
```

```
    }

    function sensitiveOperation() public onlyOwner {
        // Restricted logic
    }
}
```

Audit and Analysis Tools

Conducting audits is essential to identify vulnerabilities before deployment. Tools like MythX, Slither, and Oyente offer automated analysis to find common issues in Solidity contracts.

Updates and Mitigations

Although contracts on the blockchain are immutable, standards such as proxy allow for updates. Proxy contracts delegate calls to a logic contract, which can be overridden when necessary.

solidity

```
contract Proxy {
    address private implementation;

    function setImplementation(address newImplementation) public {
        implementation = newImplementation;
    }

    fallback() external payable {
        (bool success, ) = implementation.delegatecall(msg.data);
        require(success, "Delegatecall failed");
    }
}
```

This approach keeps the data intact while allowing you to update the logic.

Ensuring security in smart contracts is an ongoing task that requires attention to detail, rigorous testing, and adherence to best practices. Mitigating vulnerabilities such as reentrancy and overflow, implementing access controls and using auditing tools are essential steps to protect contracts against attacks. Adopting secure practices strengthens trust in the blockchain ecosystem and promotes the development of robust and innovative decentralized solutions.

CHAPTER 12. TESTING CONTRACTS

Testing smart contracts is an essential step to ensure that the logic, security, and functionality of a contract operates as expected before it is deployed on the blockchain. As contracts are immutable after deployment, any error can have serious consequences, such as financial losses or exposure to attacks. Frameworks like **Today** offer powerful tools for writing and running automated tests of smart contracts, simplifying development and validation.

This chapter covers how to set up a testing environment, write effective tests for smart contracts, and use advanced tools in **Today** to detect and correct faults.

Importance of Testing in Smart Contracts

Tests are essential to identify and correct errors in contract logic, avoid security vulnerabilities and validate functionality in different scenarios. They also ensure that the contract is compatible with customer expectations and regulatory requirements.

Key benefits of testing include:

1. **Early Error Detection**: Allows you to fix problems before deployment.
2. **Risk Reduction**: Minimizes vulnerabilities that could be exploited.
3. **Automation**: Simplifies continuous validation of

contracts with each change.

4. **Documentation**: Serves as a reference on the expected behavior of the contract.

Test Environment Configuration

Before you start writing tests, you need to set up the environment. THE **Today** is a popular choice due to its flexibility and integration with libraries such as **Chai** and **Ethers.js**.

Hardhat installation

1. Install Node.js and npm (Node Package Manager), if you don't already have it.
2. Create a directory for the project and start a Node package:

bash

```
mkdir contract-testing
cd contract-testing
npm init -y
```

3. Install o Hardhat:

bash

```
npm install --save-dev hardhat
```

4. Initialize the Hardhat project:

bash

```
npx hardhat
```

Choose the option to create a basic project.

5. Install additional dependencies for testing:

bash

npm install --save-dev @nomiclabs/hardhat-ethers ethers chai

These dependencies include tools for interacting with contracts and validating results.

Hardhat Project Structure

Hardhat organizes project files into a clear structure:

- **contracts/**: Contains Solidity contracts.
- **scripts/**: Stores scripts for deployment.
- **test/**: Where tests are written and executed.
- **hardhat.config.js**: Main configuration file.

Create a simple contract to test:

solidity

```solidity
// contracts/Counter.sol
pragma solidity ^0.8.0;

contract Counter {
    uint public count;

    function increment() public {
        count += 1;
    }

    function decrement() public {
        require(count > 0, "Counter cannot be negative");
        count -= 1;
    }
}
```

The contract Counter allows you to increment and decrement a value, with validation that prevents negative values.

Writing Tests with Hardhat

Tests in Hardhat are written in JavaScript or TypeScript and use libraries such as **Chai** for assertions.

1. Create a test file in the directory test/:

bash

```
touch test/Counter.js
```

2. Implement the tests for the contract Counter:

javascript

```
const { expect } = require("chai");
const { ethers } = require("hardhat");

describe("Counter Contract", () => {
  let Counter, counter;

  beforeEach(async () => {
    Counter = await ethers.getContractFactory("Counter");
    counter = await Counter.deploy();
    await counter.deployed();
  });

  it("should initialize with count = 0", async () => {
    expect(await counter.count()).to.equal(0);
  });

  it("should increment the count", async () => {
    await counter.increment();
    expect(await counter.count()).to.equal(1);
```

```
  });

  it("should decrement the count", async () => {
    await counter.increment();
    await counter.decrement();
    expect(await counter.count()).to.equal(0);
  });

  it("should not allow count to go below zero", async () => {
    await
expect(counter.decrement()).to.be.revertedWith("Counter
cannot be negative");
  });
});
```

The tests verify the initial state of the contract, validate increment and decrement operations, and ensure that validation to prevent negative counts works correctly.

Running the Tests

To run the tests, use the command:

bash

npx hardhat test

Hardhat will execute all files in the directory test/ and will display the results in the console.

Advanced Testing with Hardhat

Testing Events

Events are often used to record important actions. It is crucial to validate that they are being issued correctly.

Add an event to the contract Counter:

solidity

```solidity
pragma solidity ^0.8.0;

contract Counter {
    uint public count;

    event CountUpdated(uint newCount);

    function increment() public {
        count += 1;
        emit CountUpdated(count);
    }

    function decrement() public {
        require(count > 0, "Counter cannot be negative");
        count -= 1;
        emit CountUpdated(count);
    }
}
```

Update tests to check for events:

javascript

```javascript
it("should emit CountUpdated event on increment", async () => {
    await expect(counter.increment())
      .to.emit(counter, "CountUpdated")
      .withArgs(1);
});

it("should emit CountUpdated event on decrement", async () =>
{
    await counter.increment(); // Count = 1
    await expect(counter.decrement())
      .to.emit(counter, "CountUpdated")
```

```
    .withArgs(0);
});
```

Testing Asynchronous Functionality

Contracts that interact with other contracts or rely on external calls can include asynchronous logic. Simulate external contracts using **Today**.

Create a contract for interaction:

solidity

```solidity
pragma solidity ^0.8.0;

interface IExternalContract {
    function externalFunction() external returns (bool);
}

contract ExternalCaller {
    function callExternal(IExternalContract externalContract)
public returns (bool) {
        return externalContract.externalFunction();
    }
}
```

Test the interaction by simulating the external contract:

javascript

```javascript
it("should call the external contract", async () => {
    const          MockExternalContract      =           await
ethers.getContractFactory("MockExternalContract");
    const mockExternal = await MockExternalContract.deploy();
    await mockExternal.deployed();

    const ExternalCaller = await
ethers.getContractFactory("ExternalCaller");
    const caller = await ExternalCaller.deploy();
```

```
await caller.deployed();

expect(await
caller.callExternal(mockExternal.address)).to.be.true;
});
```

Testing Strategies

1. **Code Coverage**: Ensure that all functions and logical paths are tested.
2. **Limit Scenarios**: Validate extreme inputs to avoid unexpected behavior.
3. **Security Test**: Simulate attacks, such as reentrancy or overflow, to verify contract resilience.
4. **Continuous Integration**: Integrate tests into CI/CD pipelines to automatically validate code changes.

Complementary Tools

- **Coverage**: To measure test coverage.
- **Ethers.js**: Library for interacting with contracts.
- **Ganache**: Local blockchain for rapid testing.

Testing smart contracts is an essential practice to ensure the functionality, security and reliability of decentralized applications. Using tools like Hardhat simplifies the process, allowing developers to detect and fix problems efficiently. By incorporating automated testing into the workflow, it is possible to deliver contracts that meet user expectations and market demands.

CHAPTER 13. CONTRACT DEPLOYMENT

Deploying smart contracts is the final step in the development of decentralized applications (DApps). This process involves transferring the contract from the development phase to a blockchain, be it a testnet for validation or a mainnet for public use. Contract implementation requires a clear understanding of the tools, associated costs, and steps to ensure successful execution. This chapter covers how to deploy on Ethereum networks, using tools such as **MetaMask**, **Today** and test networks like **Goerli**.

Contract Deployment Fundamentals

Deploying a smart contract involves publishing the contract's compiled code to the blockchain. This process requires:

1. **Compilation**: Transform Solidity code into bytecode executable by the Ethereum Virtual Machine (EVM).
2. **Interaction with Blockchain**: Use a wallet or tool to send transactions that contain the contract bytecode.
3. **Gas Taxes**: Pay for the computing resources required for deployment.

After deployment, the contract gains a unique address on the blockchain, allowing users and other applications to interact with it.

Redes de Teste vs. Mainnets

Before deploying to a mainnet, such as Ethereum, it is recommended to carry out testing on testnets. Testnets simulate the mainnet environment, but use fictitious tokens, allowing experimentation without real costs.

Popular test networks include:

- **Goerli**: One of the main Ethereum testnets, used widely by the community.
- **Sepolia**: Another lightweight and efficient test network.
- **Localhost (Blockchain Local)**: Simulations carried out with tools such as **Ganache** or **Hardhat Network**.

Testnets help identify and correct errors, validate features and simulate interactions before official deployment.

Initial Configuration for Deploy

Hardhat Configuration

Hardhat is a powerful tool for developing and deploying smart contracts. It easily integrates with Ethereum networks and wallets like MetaMask.

    1. Install o Hardhat no project:

bash

```
npm install --save-dev hardhat
```

    2. Configure connection to Ethereum networks in the file hardhat.config.js:

javascript

```
require("@nomiclabs/hardhat-ethers");

module.exports = {
  solidity: "0.8.0",
  networks: {
    goerli: {
      url: "https://goerli.infura.io/v3/
YOUR_INFURA_PROJECT_ID",
      accounts: ["YOUR_PRIVATE_KEY"],
    },
    sepolia: {
      url: "https://sepolia.infura.io/v3/
YOUR_INFURA_PROJECT_ID",
      accounts: ["YOUR_PRIVATE_KEY"],
    },
  },
};
```

Replace YOUR_INFURA_PROJECT_ID by project ID on the platform **Fat** (or similar) and YOUR_PRIVATE_KEY by the private key of the wallet that will execute the deployment.

MetaMask Configuration

MetaMask is a widely used browser extension for interacting with DApps and transacting on Ethereum networks. It works as a bridge between the developer and the blockchain.

1. Install the MetaMask extension and create a wallet.
2. Configure the test network in MetaMask:
   ○ Access **Settings** > **Networks**.
   ○ Add a custom network with the following details for Goerli:
     ■ **Network Name**: Goerli Testnet
     ■ **URL RPC**: https://goerli.infura.io/v3/

YOUR_INFURA_PROJECT_ID
- **Chain ID**: 5
- **Symbol**: ETH
- **Explorer**: https://goerli.etherscan.io

3. Get test tokens (Goerli ETH) from faucets like faucet.paradigm.xyz.

Deployment Process with Hardhat

1. Writing the Contract

Create a simple contract:

solidity

```solidity
// contracts/HelloWorld.sol
pragma solidity ^0.8.0;

contract HelloWorld {
    string public message;

    constructor(string memory _message) {
        message = _message;
    }

    function setMessage(string memory _newMessage) public {
        message = _newMessage;
    }
}
```

2. Script de Deploy

Write a script to deploy the contract:

javascript

```javascript
// scripts/deploy.js
const { ethers } = require("hardhat");

async function main() {
```

```
  const HelloWorld = await
ethers.getContractFactory("HelloWorld");
  const helloWorld = await HelloWorld.deploy("Hello,
Blockchain!");
  await helloWorld.deployed();

  console.log("Contract deployed to:", helloWorld.address);
}

main().catch((error) => {
  console.error(error);
  process.exitCode = 1;
});
```

3. Running the Deploy

To deploy the contract on the Goerli network:

bash

```
npx hardhat run scripts/deploy.js --network goerli
```

Hardhat will display the address of the deployed contract.

Interaction with the Contract

After deployment, interact with the contract using **ethers.js** or **MetaMask**.

Using ethers.js

Write a script to call contract functions:

javascript

```
const { ethers } = require("hardhat");

async function main() {
  const contractAddress = "DEPLOYED_CONTRACT_ADDRESS";
```

```javascript
const abi = [
  "function message() public view returns (string memory)",
  "function setMessage(string memory _newMessage) public",
];

const provider = new
ethers.providers.JsonRpcProvider("https://goerli.infura.io/v3/
YOUR_INFURA_PROJECT_ID");
const wallet = new ethers.Wallet("YOUR_PRIVATE_KEY",
provider);
const contract = new ethers.Contract(contractAddress, abi,
wallet);

console.log("Current message:", await contract.message());

const tx = await contract.setMessage("Hello, Ethereum!");
await tx.wait();

console.log("Updated message:", await contract.message());
}

main().catch((error) => {
  console.error(error);
  process.exitCode = 1;
});
```

Using MetaMask

1. Access Remix and import the contract.
2. Connect MetaMask to Remix and interact with the deployed contract using its interface.

Gas Costs and Optimization

The implementation cost depends on the size of the contract and the complexity of its logic. To reduce costs:

1. **Optimize the Code**: Use good coding practices to avoid unnecessary operations.
2. **Use Compactors**: Compress the contract bytecode before deploying.
3. **Track Gas Prices**: Use tools like https://ethgasstation.info/ to choose times with lower rates.

Good Practices in Deployment

- **Perform Extensive Testing**: Before deploying to a mainnet, test rigorously on test networks.
- **Validate Addresses and Data**: Check that the data provided is correct and the addresses are valid.
- **Use Secure Accounts**: Protect the private keys used in the deployment process.
- **Audit the Contract**: Perform security audits to identify vulnerabilities.
- **Document the Process**: Record the deployment details for future reference.

Deploying smart contracts is a critical process in the DApp development cycle. Using tools such as Hardhat and MetaMask, together with good practices, ensures that the contract is implemented in an efficient, safe and functional way. By mastering the deployment process, developers are ready to deliver decentralized solutions that meet market demands and provide real value to users.

CHAPTER 14. INTERACTION WITH DAPPS

The interaction between smart contracts and frontend interfaces is one of the pillars of the decentralized applications (dApps) ecosystem. A dApp combines the functionality of smart contracts with user-friendly interfaces so that users can interact simply and efficiently with the blockchain. This communication is mediated by libraries such as **Web3.js** and **Ethers.js**, which allow the connection between the frontend and smart contracts, in addition to managing transactions, querying on-chain data and integrating digital wallets like MetaMask.

This chapter explores how to create the interaction between smart contracts and dApps, covering everything from initial configuration to executing transactions and queries to the blockchain.

Fundamentals of Frontend-Blockchain Communication

A typical dApp consists of:

1. **Frontend**: Graphical interface developed with frameworks such as React, Angular or Vue.js.
2. **Communication Library**: Tools like **Web3.js** or **Ethers.js** to interact with smart contracts.
3. **Smart Contract**: Code implemented in Solidity and deployed on a public or private blockchain.
4. **Provider**: A blockchain node, such as Infura or Alchemy, that allows the frontend to connect to the

network.

The basic communication flow involves:

- **Provider**: The frontend uses libraries to connect to the provider.
- **Contract**: Libraries interact with smart contract methods.
- **Response**: Transaction data or results are returned to the frontend.

Initial Setup

Development Environment

Before you begin, set up a development environment that includes:

- **Node.js e npm**: To manage packages and run scripts.
- **React ou Framework Similar**: To develop the frontend.
- **Communication Library**: Install **Web3.js** or **Ethers.js**.

Create a new React project:

bash

```
npx create-react-app my-dapp
cd my-dapp
npm install ethers web3
```

Smart Contract for Testing

Use a basic contract to illustrate the interaction:

solidity

```
// contracts/SimpleStorage.sol
pragma solidity ^0.8.0;

contract SimpleStorage {
    uint public storedValue;

    function setValue(uint value) public {
        storedValue = value;
    }

    function getValue() public view returns (uint) {
        return storedValue;
    }
}
```

Deploy the contract to a testnet, such as Goerli, using Hardhat or Truffle.

Connection to the Provider

Add MetaMask integration to connect the dApp to the blockchain:

javascript

```javascript
async function connectWallet() {
  if (window.ethereum) {
    try {
      await window.ethereum.request({ method:
'eth_requestAccounts' });
      console.log("Wallet connected");
    } catch (error) {
      console.error("User denied wallet connection");
    }
  } else {
    console.error("MetaMask not detected");
  }
```

```
}
```

Call this function when clicking a button in the frontend to sign in the user.

Using Web3.js for Interaction

Connection to Contract

Configure the provider and connect to the contract:

javascript

```javascript
import Web3 from "web3";

const web3 = new Web3(window.ethereum);

const contractAddress = "DEPLOYED_CONTRACT_ADDRESS";
const abi = [
  {
    "constant": true,
    "inputs": [],
    "name": "storedValue",
    "outputs": [{ "name": "", "type": "uint256" }],
    "payable": false,
    "stateMutability": "view",
    "type": "function",
  },
  {
    "constant": false,
    "inputs": [{ "name": "value", "type": "uint256" }],
    "name": "setValue",
    "outputs": [],
    "payable": false,
    "stateMutability": "nonpayable",
    "type": "function",
  },
```

```
];

const contract = new web3.eth.Contract(abi, contractAddress);
```

Reading Calls

To query contract data, use methods call:

javascript

```
async function getStoredValue() {
  const value = await contract.methods.storedValue().call();
  console.log("Stored Value:", value);
}
```

Transactions

Submit transactions to change the contract state:

javascript

```
async function setStoredValue(value) {
  const accounts = await web3.eth.getAccounts();
  await contract.methods.setValue(value).send({ from:
accounts[0] });
  console.log("Value updated");
}
```

Using Ethers.js for Interaction

Connection to Contract

THE **Ethers.js** provides a simpler and more efficient API for interacting with smart contracts:

javascript

```
import { ethers } from "ethers";

const provider = new
```

```
ethers.providers.Web3Provider(window.ethereum);
const signer = provider.getSigner();

const contractAddress = "DEPLOYED_CONTRACT_ADDRESS";
const abi = [
  "function storedValue() view returns (uint256)",
  "function setValue(uint256 value)",
];

const contract = new ethers.Contract(contractAddress, abi,
signer);
```

Reading Calls

Use methods call To consult the contract:

javascript

```
async function getStoredValue() {
  const value = await contract.storedValue();
  console.log("Stored Value:", value);
}
```

Transactions

Send transactions with signer:

javascript

```
async function setStoredValue(value) {
  const tx = await contract.setValue(value);
  await tx.wait();
  console.log("Transaction confirmed");
}
```

Complete Frontend Integration

Create a simple interface to interact with the contract:

React components

javascript

```javascript
import React, { useState } from "react";
import { ethers } from "ethers";

function App() {
  const [storedValue, setStoredValue] = useState(0);
  const [newValue, setNewValue] = useState("");

  const provider = new
ethers.providers.Web3Provider(window.ethereum);
  const signer = provider.getSigner();

  const contractAddress = "DEPLOYED_CONTRACT_ADDRESS";
  const abi = [
    "function storedValue() view returns (uint256)",
    "function setValue(uint256 value)",
  ];
  const contract = new ethers.Contract(contractAddress, abi,
signer);

  async function fetchStoredValue() {
    const value = await contract.storedValue();
    setStoredValue(value.toString());
  }

  async function updateStoredValue() {
    const tx = await contract.setValue(newValue);
    await tx.wait();
    setNewValue("");
    fetchStoredValue();
  }

  return (
    <div>
      <h1>Simple Storage</h1>
```

```
    <p>Stored Value: {storedValue}</p>
    <button onClick={fetchStoredValue}>Fetch Value</
button>
    <input
     type="number"
     value={newValue}
     onChange={(e) => setNewValue(e.target.value)}
    />
    <button onClick={updateStoredValue}>Update Value</
button>
   </div>
  );
}

export default App;
```

State and Security Management

1. **Input Validation**: Always validate user input to avoid invalid data or exploits.
2. **User Feedback**: Display messages about transaction status and errors.
3. **Security**: Never store private keys in the frontend.

Good Practices

- **Contract Audit**: Ensure that deployed contracts are secure.
- **Intuitive interface**: Create a clear and efficient user experience.
- **Redundancy**: Configure backup providers to avoid connection failures.

Connecting smart contracts to frontend interfaces is the final step to creating functional and accessible dApps. With libraries like **Web3.js** and **Ethers.js**, it is possible to integrate contracts with ease, ensuring that users can interact with the blockchain in a fluid and secure way. Understanding these tools and practices prepares developers to deliver robust decentralized solutions that transform the user experience in the blockchain ecosystem.

CHAPTER 15. ERC-20: CREATING FUNGIBLE TOKENS

The ERC-20 standard is one of the pillars of the blockchain ecosystem, providing a common basis for creating fungible tokens on Ethereum. These tokens are widely used in decentralized finance (DeFi), tokenization markets and blockchain games. This standard defines a set of functions and events that ensure interoperability between smart contracts, wallets and exchanges.

This chapter details how to create an ERC-20 token, implement essential functions such as transfer and approve, and explore best practices to optimize safety and efficiency.

Introduction to the ERC-20 Standard

The ERC-20 standard has been proposed as a standard interface for fungible tokens. This means that each unit of the token is indistinguishable from another, similar to fiat currencies like dollars or euros. The standard defines six mandatory functions and two events to enable basic token transfer and tracking functionality.

Mandatory Functions

1. totalSupply: Returns the total number of existing tokens.
2. balanceOf: Returns the balance of a specific address.
3. transfer: Transfers tokens from the sender to another address.

4. transferFrom: Allows transfers between third parties, provided there is authorization.
5. approve: Authorizes an address to spend tokens on the owner's behalf.
6. allowance: Returns the number of tokens an address is authorized to spend.

Events

1. Transfer: Issued whenever tokens are transferred.
2. Approval: Issued when an authorization is granted.

Creating an ERC-20 Token

Basic Structure

Below is the basic implementation of an ERC-20 token:

solidity

```solidity
// SPDX-License-Identifier: MIT
pragma solidity ^0.8.0;

contract MyToken {
    string public name = "MyToken";
    string public symbol = "MTK";
    uint8 public decimals = 18;
    uint256 public totalSupply;

    mapping(address => uint256) public balanceOf;
    mapping(address => mapping(address => uint256)) public
allowance;

    event Transfer(address indexed from, address indexed to,
uint256 value);
    event Approval(address indexed owner, address indexed
spender, uint256 value);
```

```solidity
    constructor(uint256 _initialSupply) {
        totalSupply = _initialSupply * (10 ** uint256(decimals));
        balanceOf[msg.sender] = totalSupply;
        emit Transfer(address(0), msg.sender, totalSupply);
    }

    function transfer(address _to, uint256 _value) public returns
(bool success) {
        require(balanceOf[msg.sender] >= _value, "Insufficient
balance");
        balanceOf[msg.sender] -= _value;
        balanceOf[_to] += _value;
        emit Transfer(msg.sender, _to, _value);
        return true;
    }

    function approve(address _spender, uint256 _value) public
returns (bool success) {
        allowance[msg.sender][_spender] = _value;
        emit Approval(msg.sender, _spender, _value);
        return true;
    }

    function transferFrom(address _from, address _to, uint256
_value) public returns (bool success) {
        require(balanceOf[_from] >= _value, "Insufficient
balance");
        require(allowance[_from][msg.sender] >= _value,
"Allowance exceeded");
        balanceOf[_from] -= _value;
        balanceOf[_to] += _value;
        allowance[_from][msg.sender] -= _value;
        emit Transfer(_from, _to, _value);
        return true;
    }
}
```

Explanation of the Code

1. **Builder**: Initializes the contract with the name, symbol, number of decimals, and total token supply.
2. transfer: Performs direct transfers of tokens between addresses.
3. approve: Allows an address to spend tokens on behalf of the owner.
4. transferFrom: Uses authorization approve to transfer tokens between third parties.

Advanced Functions

Function allowance

The function allowance is used to check the number of tokens that one address is authorized to spend on behalf of another.

solidity

```solidity
function allowance(address _owner, address _spender) public
view returns (uint256 remaining) {
    return allowance[_owner][_spender];
}
```

Issuing Tokens

In many cases, ERC-20 contracts allow the issuance of new tokens. This can be done with a function as:

solidity

```solidity
function mint(address _to, uint256 _value) public {
    totalSupply += _value;
    balanceOf[_to] += _value;
    emit Transfer(address(0), _to, _value);
}
```

Issuing new tokens should be used with caution as it can affect the value and trust in the token.

Token Burn

Burning tokens reduces the total in circulation, increasing the value of remaining units:

solidity

```solidity
function burn(uint256 _value) public {
    require(balanceOf[msg.sender] >= _value, "Insufficient balance");
    balanceOf[msg.sender] -= _value;
    totalSupply -= _value;
    emit Transfer(msg.sender, address(0), _value);
}
```

Implementing Security

Overflow and Underflow Prevention

With modern versions of Solidity (>= 0.8.0), overflow and underflow are automatically prevented. However, in older versions, libraries like SafeMath are essential.

solidity

```solidity
using SafeMath for uint256;
```

Address Validation

Always check that the destination address is valid to avoid transfers to address zero:

solidity

```solidity
require(_to != address(0), "Invalid address");
```

Access Control

Implement access control on sensitive functions such as as, to avoid abuse:

solidity

```solidity
address public owner;

modifier onlyOwner() {
    require(msg.sender == owner, "Access denied");
    _;
}

constructor() {
    owner = msg.sender;
}

function mint(address _to, uint256 _value) public onlyOwner {
    totalSupply += _value;
    balanceOf[_to] += _value;
    emit Transfer(address(0), _to, _value);
}
```

Testing the Token

Before deploying the contract, perform comprehensive testing on test networks like Goerli.

Testando com Hardhat

Write automated tests to ensure functionality:

javascript

```javascript
const { expect } = require("chai");
```

```
const { ethers } = require("hardhat");

describe("MyToken", function () {
  let Token, token, owner, addr1, addr2;

  beforeEach(async function () {
    Token = await ethers.getContractFactory("MyToken");
    [owner, addr1, addr2] = await ethers.getSigners();
    token = await Token.deploy(1000);
    await token.deployed();
  });

  it("Should assign the total supply to the owner", async
function () {
    expect(await
token.balanceOf(owner.address)).to.equal(ethers.utils.parseUni
ts("1000", 18));
  });

  it("Should transfer tokens between accounts", async function
() {
    await token.transfer(addr1.address, 50);
    expect(await token.balanceOf(addr1.address)).to.equal(50);
  });

  it("Should approve and transfer tokens via transferFrom",
async function () {
    await token.approve(addr1.address, 100);
    await token.connect(addr1).transferFrom(owner.address,
addr2.address, 50);
    expect(await token.balanceOf(addr2.address)).to.equal(50);
  });
});
```

Deployment and Use

Deploy com Hardhat

Use the deploy script to deploy the contract:

javascript

```javascript
const { ethers } = require("hardhat");

async function main() {
  const Token = await ethers.getContractFactory("MyToken");
  const token = await Token.deploy(1000);
  await token.deployed();

  console.log("Token deployed to:", token.address);
}

main().catch((error) => {
  console.error(error);
  process.exitCode = 1;
});
```

Execute o script:

bash

```bash
npx hardhat run scripts/deploy.js --network goerli
```

Interaction with Ethers.js

Interact with the contract using Ethers.js:

javascript

```javascript
const contract = new ethers.Contract(contractAddress, abi, signer);

async function getBalance(address) {
  const balance = await contract.balanceOf(address);
  console.log("Balance:", ethers.utils.formatUnits(balance, 18));
}
```

```
async function sendTokens(to, amount) {
  const tx = await contract.transfer(to,
ethers.utils.parseUnits(amount, 18));
  await tx.wait();
  console.log("Tokens sent");
}
```

Creating ERC-20 tokens is a fundamental component of development on Ethereum, providing a standardized framework for interoperability. Implementing essential functions, optimizing security, and performing comprehensive testing ensure tokens are functional, secure, and compatible with the ecosystem. The creation of robust and reliable tokens allows the development of innovative solutions that harness the potential of blockchain.

CHAPTER 16. ERC-721: CREATING NFTS

The ERC-721 standard is the foundation for non-fungible tokens (NFTs) in the Ethereum ecosystem. Unlike fungible tokens (ERC-20), where each unit is indistinguishable from another, NFTs are unique and can represent ownership of digital or physical items such as works of art, music, real estate and more. This standard defines a set of functionalities that allow the creation and management of unique and traceable assets on the blockchain.

In this chapter, we will explore the ERC-721 standard, how to implement NFTs in Solidity, and the practical uses of these technologies, from blockchain-based games to digital marketplaces.

The ERC-721 Standard

ERC-721 defines an interface for non-fungible tokens. It ensures interoperability between different smart contracts and applications that deal with NFTs. The standard includes functionality for transferring, tracking, and querying token properties.

Essential Functions and Events

1. **Mandatory Functions**:
   o   balanceOf: Returns the number of NFTs owned by an address.
   o   ownerOf: Returns the owner of a specific token.
   o   safeTransferFrom: Transfers a token to another

address securely.

- ○ **transferFrom**: Transfers a token without performing additional checks.
- ○ **approve**: Authorizes another address to transfer a token on behalf of the owner.
- ○ **setApprovalForAll**: Authorizes or revokes an operator's permission to manage all of the owner's tokens.
- ○ **getApproved**: Returns the approved address for a specific token.
- ○ **isApprovedForAll**: Checks whether an operator is authorized for all of an owner's tokens.

2. **Events**:
- ○ **Transfer**: Issued when a token is transferred.
- ○ **Approval**: Issued when a token is approved for transfer.
- ○ **ApprovalForAll**: Issued when an operator is authorized or revoked.

Implementing an ERC-721 Agreement

Basic Contract Structure

To implement an ERC-721 token, you can use the OpenZeppelin library, which provides a robust and secure implementation of the standard.

solidity

```
// SPDX-License-Identifier: MIT
pragma solidity ^0.8.0;

import "@openzeppelin/contracts/token/ERC721/ERC721.sol";

contract MyNFT is ERC721 {
    uint256 public nextTokenId;
    address public admin;
```

```
constructor() ERC721("MyNFT", "MNFT") {
    admin = msg.sender;
}

function mint(address to) external {
    require(msg.sender == admin, "Only admin can mint");
    _safeMint(to, nextTokenId);
    nextTokenId++;
}

function _baseURI() internal view override returns (string
memory) {
    return "https://api.mynft.com/metadata/";
}
}
```

Explanation of the Code

1. **ERC721**: The base class provided by OpenZeppelin implements all the mandatory functionalities of the ERC-721 standard.
2. **Builder**: Sets the token name and symbol.
3. **as**: Allows the administrator to create new tokens.
4. **_baseURI**: Defines the base URL for NFT metadata.

Advanced Functions

Customizing Metadata

NFTs often have metadata that describes their properties, such as name, image, and attributes. This data is stored outside of the blockchain (usually in systems like IPFS) and referenced via a URL.

Add support for custom metadata:

solidity

```solidity
mapping(uint256 => string) private _tokenURIs;

function setTokenURI(uint256 tokenId, string memory
_tokenURI) public {
    require(_exists(tokenId), "Token does not exist");
    require(msg.sender == admin, "Only admin can set
metadata");
    _tokenURIs[tokenId] = _tokenURI;
}

function tokenURI(uint256 tokenId) public view override
returns (string memory) {
    require(_exists(tokenId), "Token does not exist");
    return _tokenURIs[tokenId];
}
```

Implementing Royalties

Add support for royalties so creators receive a percentage of each subsequent sale:

solidity

```solidity
mapping(uint256 => uint256) public royalties;

function setRoyalty(uint256 tokenId, uint256
royaltyPercentage) public {
    require(msg.sender == admin, "Only admin can set royalty");
    royalties[tokenId] = royaltyPercentage;
}

function getRoyaltyInfo(uint256 tokenId, uint256 salePrice)
public view returns (uint256) {
    return (salePrice * royalties[tokenId]) / 100;
}
```

Marketplaces can consult getRoyaltyInfo to calculate the royalties to be paid to the creator.

Testing the Contract

Use tools like Hardhat to test the contract.

Script de Deploy

Create a script to deploy the contract:

javascript

```javascript
const { ethers } = require("hardhat");

async function main() {
  const MyNFT = await ethers.getContractFactory("MyNFT");
  const myNFT = await MyNFT.deploy();
  await myNFT.deployed();
  console.log("Contract deployed to:", myNFT.address);
}

main().catch((error) => {
  console.error(error);
  process.exitCode = 1;
});
```

Automated Tests

Implement tests to validate functionalities:

javascript

```javascript
const { expect } = require("chai");

describe("MyNFT", function () {
  let MyNFT, myNFT, admin, addr1;
```

```
beforeEach(async function () {
  MyNFT = await ethers.getContractFactory("MyNFT");
  [admin, addr1] = await ethers.getSigners();
  myNFT = await MyNFT.deploy();
  await myNFT.deployed();
});

it("Should mint a new NFT", async function () {
  await myNFT.mint(addr1.address);
  expect(await myNFT.balanceOf(addr1.address)).to.equal(1);
});

it("Should set and get token URI", async function () {
  await myNFT.mint(addr1.address);
  await myNFT.setTokenURI(0, "https://example.com/
metadata/0");
  expect(await myNFT.tokenURI(0)).to.equal("https://
example.com/metadata/0");
});

it("Should calculate royalties correctly", async function () {
  await myNFT.mint(addr1.address);
  await myNFT.setRoyalty(0, 10); // 10%
  const royalty = await myNFT.getRoyaltyInfo(0, 1000); // Sale
price: 1000
  expect(royalty).to.equal(100);
});
});
```

Applications and Uses of NFTs

1. **Digital Art**: Representation of exclusive works of art, guaranteeing authenticity and ownership.
2. **Games**: In-game items such as weapons and skins can be represented as NFTs.
3. **Certificates and Identity**: NFTs can be used for

educational certificates, event tickets, and digital identities.

4. **Real Estate**: Representation of physical properties to facilitate transfers and tracking.

Good Practices

- **Conformity**: Follow ERC-721 standards to ensure interoperability.
- **Decentralized Metadata**: Use IPFS to store metadata, ensuring availability.
- **Scalability**: Consider optimizations for contracts that manage a large number of NFTs.
- **Security Audit**: NFT contracts must be audited to avoid vulnerabilities.

The ERC-721 standard opened new horizons in the use of blockchain, enabling the creation and management of unique digital assets. From digital collectibles to practical applications in identity and real estate, NFTs have transformed the way we understand property and value. Implementing an ERC-721 contract following best practices ensures not only functionality, but also security and compatibility with the growing NFT ecosystem.

CHAPTER 17. ERC-1155: MULTIMODALITY TOKENS

The ERC-1155 standard, introduced by Enjin, is a significant evolution in token standards on the Ethereum blockchain. It combines the functionality of fungible (like ERC-20) and non-fungible (like ERC-721) tokens into a single smart contract. This allows you to create diverse collections of digital assets such as coins, game items and NFTs in an efficient and scalable way.

With ERC-1155, developers can manage multiple types of tokens with a single contract, reducing gas costs and simplifying collection management. This chapter explores the fundamentals of the pattern, its unique features, and how to use it to create practical applications.

ERC-1155 Fundamentals

ERC-1155 introduces an innovative approach to creating and managing tokens:

- **Multimodality**: A contract can contain multiple types of tokens, each identified by a unique ID.
- **Bulk Transfer**: Allows you to transfer multiple types and quantities of tokens in a single transaction, saving gas.
- **Interoperability**: Combines the benefits of ERC-20 and ERC-721 standards, maintaining compatibility with wallets and marketplaces.

Main Functions and Events

1. **Mandatory Functions**:
   - balanceOf: Returns the balance of a token type for an address.
   - balanceOfBatch: Returns the balances of multiple token types for multiple addresses.
   - safeTransferFrom: Transfers tokens of one type to another address.
   - safeBatchTransferFrom: Transfer multiple types of tokens in a single operation.
   - setApprovalForAll: Authorizes or revokes permission for an operator to manage owner tokens.
   - isApprovedForAll: Checks whether an operator is authorized to manage tokens for an address.
2. **Events**:
   - TransferSingle: Issued for a transfer of a single token type.
   - TransferBatch: Issued for transfers of multiple token types.
   - ApprovalForAll: Issued when an operator is authorized or revoked.

Implementing an ERC-1155 Agreement

Basic Structure

To library **OpenZeppelin** provides a solid, tested implementation of ERC-1155.

solidity

```solidity
// SPDX-License-Identifier: MIT
pragma solidity ^0.8.0;

import "@openzeppelin/contracts/token/ERC1155/
ERC1155.sol";

contract MyMultiToken is ERC1155 {
    uint256 public constant GOLD = 1;
```

```solidity
    uint256 public constant SILVER = 2;
    uint256 public constant DIAMOND = 3;

    constructor() ERC1155("https://api.mytoken.com/
metadata/{id}.json") {
        _mint(msg.sender, GOLD, 1000, "");
        _mint(msg.sender, SILVER, 5000, "");
        _mint(msg.sender, DIAMOND, 10, "");
    }
}
```

Explanation of the Code

1. **Unified IDs**: Each token type is identified by an ID (GOLD, SILVER, DIAMOND).
2. **Builder**: Sets the base URL for the metadata and min initial amounts of each token type.
3. **Dynamic Metadata**: The format {id} in the URL allows you to link specific metadata to each token.

Advanced Features

Bulk Transfer

ERC-1155 allows you to transfer multiple types of tokens in a single transaction, reducing gas costs.

solidity

```solidity
function batchTransfer(
    address to,
    uint256[] memory ids,
    uint256[] memory amounts
) public {
    _safeBatchTransferFrom(msg.sender, to, ids, amounts, "");
}
```

Token Burn

Tokens can be burned to reduce the total in circulation:

solidity

```solidity
function burn(
    address from,
    uint256 id,
    uint256 amount
) public {
    require(from == msg.sender || isApprovedForAll(from,
msg.sender), "Not authorized");
    _burn(from, id, amount);
}
```

Custom Metadata

Add support for unique metadata for each token type:

solidity

```solidity
mapping(uint256 => string) private _customURIs;

function setTokenURI(uint256 id, string memory newURI)
public {
    _customURIs[id] = newURI;
}

function uri(uint256 id) public view override returns (string
memory) {
    return _customURIs[id];
}
```

Practical Applications

Blockchain Games

ERC-1155 is widely used in games to represent items, currencies, and characters. For example, a game might use different IDs to represent swords, armor, and gold coins.

solidity

```
contract GameItems is ERC1155 {
    uint256 public constant SWORD = 1;
    uint256 public constant SHIELD = 2;
    uint256 public constant POTION = 3;

    constructor() ERC1155("https://gameitems.example/api/
item/{id}.json") {
        _mint(msg.sender, SWORD, 100, "");
        _mint(msg.sender, SHIELD, 50, "");
        _mint(msg.sender, POTION, 200, "");
    }
}
```

Arte Marketplaces

Create a marketplace to sell limited editions of digital artworks, where each edition is represented by an ID.

solidity

```
contract ArtMarketplace is ERC1155 {
    uint256 public nextTokenId;

    function mintEdition(uint256 amount) public {
        _mint(msg.sender, nextTokenId, amount, "");
        nextTokenId++;
    }
}
```

Finance DeFi

Use ERC-1155 to represent liquidity positions or tokenized assets.

solidity

```solidity
contract LiquidityPositions is ERC1155 {
    mapping(uint256 => uint256) public poolBalances;

    function mintPosition(uint256 poolId, uint256 amount)
public {
        _mint(msg.sender, poolId, amount, "");
        poolBalances[poolId] += amount;
    }

    function burnPosition(uint256 poolId, uint256 amount)
public {
        _burn(msg.sender, poolId, amount);
        poolBalances[poolId] -= amount;
    }
}
```

Security and Good Practices

1. **Access Control**: Implement modifiers for sensitive functions such as as.
2. **Input Validation**: Verify that IDs and quantities are valid before performing operations.
3. **Code Audit**: Perform regular audits to identify vulnerabilities.
4. **Immutable Metadata**: Use decentralized systems like IPFS to ensure metadata integrity.

Testing the Contract

Use tools like Hardhat to validate contract behavior.

Transfer Test

javascript

```javascript
const { expect } = require("chai");
```

```
describe("MyMultiToken", function () {
  let MultiToken, multiToken, owner, addr1;

  beforeEach(async function () {
    MultiToken = await
ethers.getContractFactory("MyMultiToken");
    [owner, addr1] = await ethers.getSigners();
    multiToken = await MultiToken.deploy();
    await multiToken.deployed();
  });

  it("Should transfer multiple token types", async function () {
    await multiToken.safeBatchTransferFrom(
      owner.address,
      addr1.address,
      [1, 2],
      [10, 20],
      []
    );

    const balanceGold = await
multiToken.balanceOf(addr1.address, 1);
    const balanceSilver = await
multiToken.balanceOf(addr1.address, 2);

    expect(balanceGold).to.equal(10);
    expect(balanceSilver).to.equal(20);
  });
});
```

The ERC-1155 standard offers an efficient and scalable approach to managing multiple types of tokens in a single smart contract. With its versatility, it allows you to create innovative applications in games, art marketplaces, decentralized finance and much more. Adopting good security practices and implementing advanced functionalities ensures that contracts meet market demands, offering robust and interoperable solutions in the blockchain ecosystem.

CHAPTER 18. COMPLEX CONTRACTS AND DAO

Smart contracts play a crucial role in the blockchain ecosystem, enabling the execution of automated and decentralized operations. As use cases grow in complexity, smart contracts need to evolve to meet more advanced requirements. Among these innovations, Decentralized Autonomous Organizations (DAOs) emerge as a powerful model for collective and decentralized governance, allowing communities to make decisions without relying on intermediaries.

This chapter explores the construction of complex smart contracts, covering topics such as modular logic, advanced security, and design patterns, and introduces the fundamentals and implementation of DAOs.

Complex Contracts: Structures and Functionalities

Complex contracts combine multiple functionalities and interactions between different parts of the system. They can include features such as governance, dynamic access control, oracle integration, asset management, and more.

Modularity and Reusability

Modularity is essential for complex contracts, allowing parts of the code to be reused and updated without affecting the entire system. Implementation of modular contracts can be achieved through inheritance and interfaces.

Base Contracts

A base contract defines common functionality that can be reused by derived contracts:

solidity

```solidity
// SPDX-License-Identifier: MIT
pragma solidity ^0.8.0;

contract BaseContract {
    address public owner;

    modifier onlyOwner() {
        require(msg.sender == owner, "Not the owner");
        _;
    }

    constructor() {
        owner = msg.sender;
    }

    function transferOwnership(address newOwner) public
onlyOwner {
        owner = newOwner;
    }
}
```

Derivative Contracts

Derived contracts can extend the base contract to add specific functionality:

solidity

```solidity
// SPDX-License-Identifier: MIT
pragma solidity ^0.8.0;

import "./BaseContract.sol";
```

```solidity
contract VotingContract is BaseContract {
    struct Proposal {
        string description;
        uint voteCount;
    }

    Proposal[] public proposals;

    function createProposal(string memory description) public
onlyOwner {
        proposals.push(Proposal(description, 0));
    }

    function vote(uint proposalIndex) public {
        proposals[proposalIndex].voteCount++;
    }
}
```

Update Logic with Proxy Patterns

Smart contracts, by default, are immutable after deployment. However, proxy patterns allow you to update the logic of a contract without changing the stored data.

Proxy com Delegatecall

A proxy can delegate calls to an implementation contract:

solidity

```solidity
// SPDX-License-Identifier: MIT
pragma solidity ^0.8.0;

contract Proxy {
    address public implementation;

    function setImplementation(address newImplementation)
```

```
public {
    implementation = newImplementation;
  }

  fallback() external payable {
    (bool success, ) = implementation.delegatecall(msg.data);
    require(success, "Delegatecall failed");
  }
}
```

The proxy forwards calls to the implementing contract, allowing updates when the implemented contract address changes.

Decentralized Autonomous Organizations (DAOs)

DAOs are entities governed by smart contracts, allowing groups of individuals to make decisions collectively transparently and without intermediaries. They are widely used for managing funds, protocol governance, and community initiatives.

Components of a DAO

1. **Proposals**: Ideas or actions suggested by DAO members.
2. **Voting**: Process by which members approve or reject proposals.
3. **Execution**: Implementation of approved proposals.
4. **Token Governance**: Tokens used to vote and represent decision-making power.

Basic Implementation of a DAO

Governance Agreement

A basic DAO contract includes features for creating and voting on proposals:

solidity

```solidity
// SPDX-License-Identifier: MIT
pragma solidity ^0.8.0;

contract SimpleDAO {
    struct Proposal {
        string description;
        uint voteCount;
        bool executed;
    }

    Proposal[] public proposals;
    mapping(address => uint) public votingPower;
    mapping(uint => mapping(address => bool)) public
hasVoted;

    modifier onlyMember() {
        require(votingPower[msg.sender] > 0, "Not a member");
        _;
    }

    function addVotingPower(address member, uint power)
public {
        votingPower[member] += power;
    }

    function createProposal(string memory description) public
onlyMember {
        proposals.push(Proposal(description, 0, false));
    }

    function vote(uint proposalIndex) public onlyMember {
        require(!hasVoted[proposalIndex][msg.sender], "Already
voted");
```

```solidity
    proposals[proposalIndex].voteCount +=
votingPower[msg.sender];
    hasVoted[proposalIndex][msg.sender] = true;
  }

  function executeProposal(uint proposalIndex) public {
    Proposal storage proposal = proposals[proposalIndex];
    require(proposal.voteCount > 100, "Not enough votes");
    require(!proposal.executed, "Already executed");
    proposal.executed = true;
    // Execute proposal logic
  }
}
```

DAO Expansion with ERC-20 Tokens

ERC-20 tokens can be integrated to distribute voting power proportional to the number of tokens held:

solidity

```solidity
// SPDX-License-Identifier: MIT
pragma solidity ^0.8.0;

import "@openzeppelin/contracts/token/ERC20/ERC20.sol";

contract GovernanceToken is ERC20 {
  constructor() ERC20("GovernanceToken", "GT") {
    _mint(msg.sender, 1000000 * 10**decimals());
  }
}
```

Integrate the token with the DAO to use balances as a basis for votes:

solidity

```solidity
// SPDX-License-Identifier: MIT
pragma solidity ^0.8.0;

import "./GovernanceToken.sol";

contract TokenBasedDAO {
    GovernanceToken public governanceToken;

    struct Proposal {
        string description;
        uint voteCount;
        bool executed;
    }

    Proposal[] public proposals;
    mapping(uint => mapping(address => bool)) public
hasVoted;

    constructor(address tokenAddress) {
        governanceToken = GovernanceToken(tokenAddress);
    }

    function createProposal(string memory description) public {
        proposals.push(Proposal(description, 0, false));
    }

    function vote(uint proposalIndex) public {
        require(!hasVoted[proposalIndex][msg.sender], "Already
voted");
        uint balance = governanceToken.balanceOf(msg.sender);
        require(balance > 0, "No tokens to vote");
        proposals[proposalIndex].voteCount += balance;
        hasVoted[proposalIndex][msg.sender] = true;
    }

    function executeProposal(uint proposalIndex) public {
        Proposal storage proposal = proposals[proposalIndex];
```

```
        require(proposal.voteCount > 100, "Not enough votes");
        require(!proposal.executed, "Already executed");
        proposal.executed = true;
        // Execute proposal logic
    }
}
```

Security in Complex Contracts and DAOs

1. **Indentation Prevention**: Update states before transfers and use blocking modifiers.
2. **Limitation of Power**: Restrict access to sensitive functions with clear access controls.
3. **Code Audit**: Subject contracts to regular audits to identify vulnerabilities.
4. **Rescue Mechanisms**: Include functions to pause or stop operations in case of unexpected behavior.

Practical Applications of DAOs

1. **Protocol Governance**: DAOs manage DeFi protocols, allowing members to decide on fees, upgrades, and fund allocation.
2. **Community Financing**: Decentralized fundraising for community projects.
3. **Collective Ownership**: Sharing digital or physical properties, such as real estate and collectibles.
4. **Digital Cooperatives**: Business management through decentralized governance.

Complex smart contracts and DAOs represent the next stage in the evolution of blockchain technologies. They enable the creation of robust, scalable and democratic systems that decentralize power and automate governance processes. Implementing contracts with modular logic, advanced security standards and token integrations ensures efficiency, transparency and positive impact on the ecosystem. Mastering these technologies prepares developers to create innovative solutions that transform the way communities and organizations interact.

CHAPTER 19. CONTRACT INTEROPERABILITY

Interoperability is a fundamental element in the blockchain ecosystem, allowing smart contracts to interact with each other and with external systems. This communication capability enables the creation of complex and interconnected decentralized applications (dApps), such as decentralized exchanges, NFT markets and data oracles. This chapter explores communication between smart contracts and presents methods for integrating contracts with external APIs, using technologies such as oracles.

Communication between Smart Contracts

Smart contracts can interact with each other natively, sharing data and performing functions in a secure and reliable way. This functionality is often used in cases such as:

- **Function Call**: Contracts invoke functions from other contracts to obtain information or perform actions.
- **Inheritance and Modularity**: Contracts use functionalities defined in base contracts.
- **Design Patterns**: Contracts follow standards such as ERC-20, ERC-721 and ERC-1155 to ensure interoperability.

Basic Interaction between Contracts

To demonstrate communication between contracts, consider two contracts: a main contract that depends on data or actions from another auxiliary contract.

Auxiliary Contract

This contract provides a simple function to return a message:

solidity

```solidity
// SPDX-License-Identifier: MIT
pragma solidity ^0.8.0;

contract HelperContract {
    function getMessage() public pure returns (string memory) {
        return "Hello from HelperContract";
    }
}
```

Main Contract

The main contract uses the address of the auxiliary contract to call its function:

solidity

```solidity
// SPDX-License-Identifier: MIT
pragma solidity ^0.8.0;

interface IHelperContract {
    function getMessage() external view returns (string memory);
}

contract MainContract {
    address public helperAddress;

    constructor(address _helperAddress) {
```

```solidity
    helperAddress = _helperAddress;
  }

  function fetchMessage() public view returns (string
memory) {
      return IHelperContract(helperAddress).getMessage();
  }
}
```

In the example above, the main contract uses an interface to interact with the auxiliary contract. This ensures that interactions are compatible even if the auxiliary contract is at another address.

Transfer of Tokens between Contracts

Contracts that follow standards such as ERC-20 or ERC-721 can transfer assets between each other. A contract can receive tokens and perform actions based on those tokens.

ERC-20 Transfer Example

A contract that accepts deposits in ERC-20 tokens and keeps a record of balances:

solidity

```solidity
// SPDX-License-Identifier: MIT
pragma solidity ^0.8.0;

import "@openzeppelin/contracts/token/ERC20/IERC20.sol";

contract TokenVault {
    mapping(address => uint256) public balances;
```

```
    function depositTokens(address token, uint256 amount)
public {
        require(IERC20(token).transferFrom(msg.sender,
address(this), amount), "Transfer failed");
        balances[msg.sender] += amount;
    }

    function withdrawTokens(address token, uint256 amount)
public {
        require(balances[msg.sender] >= amount, "Insufficient
balance");
        balances[msg.sender] -= amount;
        require(IERC20(token).transfer(msg.sender, amount),
"Transfer failed");
    }
}
```

Integration with External APIs

External APIs provide real-time information to smart contracts, such as asset prices, weather conditions or sports results. Since contracts on the blockchain cannot directly access external data sources, it is necessary to use **oracles**.

The Role of Oracles

Oracles act as intermediaries between the blockchain and the outside world, bringing off-chain data to the on-chain environment. Platforms like Chainlink offer robust solutions for this integration.

Example of Using Oracles

A contract that uses an oracle to obtain the price of an asset:

Chainlink-Based Contract

solidity

```solidity
// SPDX-License-Identifier: MIT
pragma solidity ^0.8.0;

import "@chainlink/contracts/src/v0.8/interfaces/
AggregatorV3Interface.sol";

contract PriceConsumer {
    AggregatorV3Interface internal priceFeed;

    constructor(address _priceFeed) {
        priceFeed = AggregatorV3Interface(_priceFeed);
    }

    function getLatestPrice() public view returns (int256) {
        (, int256 price, , , ) = priceFeed.latestRoundData();
        return price;
    }
}
```

In this example, the contract queries a Chainlink oracle to obtain the latest price of an asset. The oracle address depends on the asset and the network used.

Integration with External Contracts Using Oracle Data

A contract that adjusts prices for your services based on oracle data:

solidity

```solidity
// SPDX-License-Identifier: MIT
pragma solidity ^0.8.0;
```

```
import "@chainlink/contracts/src/v0.8/interfaces/
AggregatorV3Interface.sol";

contract DynamicPricing {
    AggregatorV3Interface internal priceFeed;
    uint256 public servicePriceUSD = 10; // 10 USD

    constructor(address _priceFeed) {
        priceFeed = AggregatorV3Interface(_priceFeed);
    }

    function getServicePriceETH() public view returns (uint256)
{
        (, int256 price, , , ) = priceFeed.latestRoundData();
        require(price > 0, "Invalid price");
        uint256 ethPriceUSD = uint256(price);
        return (servicePriceUSD * 1e18) / ethPriceUSD; // Returns
the price in wei
    }
}
```

Challenges and Solutions

Latency

As off-chain data relies on oracles to be brought onto the blockchain, there may be a delay in updating information. Solutions:

- Configure more frequent update times.
- Use multiple oracles for redundancy.

Security

Oracles can be targets of attacks or provide manipulated data. Solutions:

- Use decentralized oracles that aggregate data from

multiple sources.

- Implement integrity checks on contracts.

Gas Costs

Calls to oracles can be costly. Solutions:

- Minimize the frequency of oracle calls.
- Store critical data in contracts and update them only when necessary.

Good Practices for Interoperability

1. **Interface Patterns**: Use standardized interfaces to ensure compatibility between contracts.
2. **Data Validation**: Always check the integrity of data returned by oracles or other contracts.
3. **Fallbacks**: Include alternative methods for managing failures in external oracles or contracts.
4. **Code Audit**: Subject contracts to regular audits to identify potential vulnerabilities.

Practical Applications

1. **Decentralized Exchanges**: Contracts that communicate to perform swaps and calculate prices dynamically.
2. **Event-Based Insurance**: Using oracles to trigger payments based on weather conditions or sporting events.
3. **Decentralized Finance (DeFi)**: Protocols that rely on updated prices for collateralized loans and settlements.
4. **Blockchain-Based Games**: Communication between contracts to create interconnected economies.

The interoperability of smart contracts and integration with external APIs are essential elements for expanding the functionalities of the blockchain ecosystem. The ability for contracts to communicate with each other and with the outside world allows for the creation of more advanced and useful decentralized applications. By adopting safe and efficient practices, developers can build interconnected systems that maximize the potential of blockchain technology, promoting innovation and reliability.

CHAPTER 20. GAS OPTIMIZATION

Gas optimization is one of the main concerns in the development of smart contracts. As each operation on a public blockchain like Ethereum has a cost in gas, optimizing consumption is essential to make contracts efficient and accessible. Reducing the cost of execution benefits both developers and users, especially in scenarios where interaction with contracts occurs with high frequency.

This chapter explores practical strategies for reducing gas consumption, analyzes the costs of Solidity operations, and presents design techniques to improve contract efficiency.

What is Gas?

Gas is a unit of measurement that represents the computational work required to perform an operation on the blockchain. Each instruction in the Ethereum Virtual Machine (EVM) consumes a specific amount of gas, and users pay for this consumption in Ether (ETH). The total cost is calculated as:

java

```
Total Cost = Gas Consumed * Gas Price
```

The price of gas is defined by the user and may vary depending on network demand. Well-designed contracts consume less gas, reducing costs for all parties involved.

Optimization Principles

1. **Minimize Storage on Blockchain**: Storage is one of the most expensive operations on Ethereum. Whenever possible, use temporary variables or local memory.
2. **Avoid Long Loops**: Loops can consume a significant amount of gas, especially if they iterate over large arrays.
3. **Reuse Code**: Reusable functions reduce logic duplication and save gas.
4. **Relocate Resources**: Free up storage space, where applicable, to reduce future costs.

Analysis of Gas Consumption in Common Operations

Operations in Solidity have variable costs depending on their impact on the state of the blockchain.

Storage Operations

- **Write to Storage**: 20,000 gas per operation.
- **Change Value in Storage**: 5,000 gas, if the key already has a stored value.
- **Erase Data from Storage**: Refund 15,000 gas.

Inefficient Example

solidity

```
mapping(address => uint) public balances;

function updateBalance(address user, uint newBalance) public {
    balances[user] = newBalance;
}
```

The mapping balances stores data directly on the blockchain, which is expensive for frequent changes.

Optimized Solution

Use local variables or events to avoid storing values permanently:

solidity

```
function processTransaction(address user, uint value) public {
    uint newBalance = balances[user] + value;
    balances[user] = newBalance; //Minimal storage update.
}
```

Memory and Stack Operations

- **Memory**: Temporary and cheaper than storage, used while performing functions.
- **Battery**: Used for local variables and quick operations. The stack is limited to 16 levels deep.

Solidity Optimization Strategies

Reducing Storage Usage

Avoid unnecessary storage upgrades. Update values only when strictly necessary.

Inefficient

solidity

```
function incrementCounter() public {
    counter += 1;
}
```

Optimized

solidity

```
function incrementCounter() public {
    uint temp = counter;
    temp += 1;
    counter = temp;
}
```

Using Optimized Data Structures

Choose data structures that suit your intended use. Arrays are more efficient for small sets, while mappings are useful for large volumes of data.

Inefficient

solidity

```
uint[] public values;

function addValue(uint value) public {
    values.push(value);
}
```

Optimized

Use events to record values without storing them permanently:

solidity

```
event ValueAdded(uint value);

function addValue(uint value) public {
    emit ValueAdded(value);
```

}

Avoiding Extensive Loops

Loops in large arrays can consume a lot of gas. Prefer chunked operations or asynchronous interactions.

Inefficient

solidity

```solidity
function sumArray(uint[] memory arr) public pure returns
(uint) {
    uint sum = 0;
    for (uint i = 0; i < arr.length; i++) {
        sum += arr[i];
    }
    return sum;
}
```

Optimized

Break operations into smaller parts:

solidity

```solidity
function partialSum(uint[] memory arr, uint start, uint end)
public pure returns (uint) {
    uint sum = 0;
    for (uint i = start; i < end; i++) {
        sum += arr[i];
    }
    return sum;
}
```

Using Pure Functions and View

Functions pure and view they do not change the state of the

blockchain, consuming less gas.

solidity

```solidity
function calculate(uint a, uint b) public pure returns (uint) {
    return a + b;
}
```

Contract Size Reduction

Larger contracts consume more gas during implementation. Reduce contract size by using external libraries or removing redundant code.

Inefficient

solidity

```solidity
contract LargeContract {
    function add(uint a, uint b) public pure returns (uint) {
        return a + b;
    }

    function multiply(uint a, uint b) public pure returns (uint) {
        return a * b;
    }
}
```

Optimized with Libraries

solidity

```solidity
library Math {
    function add(uint a, uint b) internal pure returns (uint) {
        return a + b;
    }

    function multiply(uint a, uint b) internal pure returns (uint) {
        return a * b;
```

```
    }
}

contract OptimizedContract {
    using Math for uint;

    function compute(uint a, uint b) public pure returns (uint,
uint) {
        return (a.add(b), a.multiply(b));
    }
}
```

Gas Consumption Analysis and Test

Tools like **Today**, **Truffle** and **Remix** allow you to measure and optimize gas consumption.

Test with Hardhat

Add gas consumption measurements to automated tests:

javascript

```javascript
const { expect } = require("chai");

describe("Gas Optimization", function () {
    let Contract, contract;

    beforeEach(async function () {
        Contract = await
ethers.getContractFactory("OptimizedContract");
        contract = await Contract.deploy();
    });

    it("should measure gas usage", async function () {
        const tx = await contract.compute(10, 20);
```

```
    const receipt = await tx.wait();
    console.log("Gas used:", receipt.gasUsed.toString());
  });
});
```

Design Patterns for Optimization

Advance Payment of Gas

Allow users to pay only for the gas they need for specific transactions.

solidity

```solidity
function performAction() public payable {
    require(msg.value >= gasleft(), "Insufficient gas sent");
    // Action executed
}
```

Process Fragmentation

Split intensive operations into several smaller transactions to avoid exceeding gas limits.

solidity

```solidity
uint public currentIndex;

function processBatch(uint[] memory data) public {
    uint end = currentIndex + 10;
    for (uint i = currentIndex; i < end && i < data.length; i++) {
        // Processing
    }
    currentIndex = end;
}
```

Gas optimization is essential for developing efficient and

affordable smart contracts. Understanding the costs associated with different operations and adopting strategies such as reducing storage, using pure functions and modular design are key to creating contracts that maximize efficiency and minimize costs. Additionally, using rigorous analysis and testing tools helps identify bottlenecks and implement continuous improvements. With these practices, it is possible to deliver robust and economically viable decentralized solutions.

CHAPTER 21. STAKING CONTRACTS

Staking is a central mechanism in the blockchain ecosystem, allowing users to lock up assets to support the network and receive rewards in return. This model is widely used in proof-of-stake (PoS) systems, decentralized finance (DeFi) platforms and incentive programs. Smart contracts play a crucial role in automating the staking process, ensuring security, transparency, and fair distribution of rewards.

This chapter covers the creation of staking contracts, from basic logic to more advanced systems with multiple tokens and dynamic reward calculations.

Staking Basics

Staking involves the participation of users who lock their tokens in a smart contract to fulfill a specific objective, such as validating transactions or ensuring liquidity. In return, they receive rewards, usually in the form of native tokens or other assets.

Essential Components

1. **Deposit**: User transfers tokens to the staking contract.
2. **Block**: Tokens are locked for a defined or indefinite period.
3. **Rewards**: The contract calculates and distributes rewards proportionally to the amount and time of staking.
4. **Withdrawal**: The user can withdraw the tokens and

accumulated rewards after the lock-in period.

Basic Staking Contract

Below is a simple staking contract that allows users to deposit ERC-20 tokens and receive fixed rewards.

solidity

```solidity
// SPDX-License-Identifier: MIT
pragma solidity ^0.8.0;

import "@openzeppelin/contracts/token/ERC20/IERC20.sol";

contract SimpleStaking {
    IERC20 public stakingToken;
    IERC20 public rewardToken;
    uint256 public rewardRate; // Reward per second
    mapping(address => uint256) public stakedAmount;
    mapping(address => uint256) public rewardDebt;
    mapping(address => uint256) public lastUpdate;

    constructor(address _stakingToken, address _rewardToken,
uint256 _rewardRate) {
        stakingToken = IERC20(_stakingToken);
        rewardToken = IERC20(_rewardToken);
        rewardRate = _rewardRate;
    }

    function stake(uint256 amount) public {
        require(amount > 0, "Amount must be greater than 0");
        updateRewards(msg.sender);
        stakingToken.transferFrom(msg.sender, address(this),
amount);
        stakedAmount[msg.sender] += amount;
    }

    function withdraw(uint256 amount) public {
        require(stakedAmount[msg.sender] >= amount,
```

```
"Insufficient staked amount");
    updateRewards(msg.sender);
    stakedAmount[msg.sender] -= amount;
    stakingToken.transfer(msg.sender, amount);
}

function claimRewards() public {
    updateRewards(msg.sender);
    uint256 rewards = rewardDebt[msg.sender];
    require(rewards > 0, "No rewards to claim");
    rewardDebt[msg.sender] = 0;
    rewardToken.transfer(msg.sender, rewards);
}

function updateRewards(address user) internal {
    uint256 timeElapsed = block.timestamp -
lastUpdate[user];
    rewardDebt[user] += stakedAmount[user] * rewardRate *
timeElapsed;
    lastUpdate[user] = block.timestamp;
}
}
```

Explanation of the Code

1. **Staking and Reward Tokens**: The contract supports two tokens: one for staking and one for rewards.
2. **Reward Calculation**: Rewards are calculated based on staking time and reward rate.
3. **Staking and Withdrawal Functions**: Users can deposit and withdraw tokens, with rewards being updated automatically.
4. **Reward Redemption**: Users can claim accumulated rewards at any time.

Adding Advanced Features

Dynamic Rewards

Instead of a fixed rate, rewards can be dynamically adjusted based on demand or market behavior.

solidity

```solidity
function setRewardRate(uint256 newRate) public onlyOwner {
    rewardRate = newRate;
}
```

Lockout Period

Implement a minimum lock-in period to prevent immediate withdrawals after staking.

solidity

```solidity
mapping(address => uint256) public lockEndTime;

function stake(uint256 amount) public {
    require(amount > 0, "Amount must be greater than 0");
    updateRewards(msg.sender);
    stakingToken.transferFrom(msg.sender, address(this), amount);
    stakedAmount[msg.sender] += amount;
    lockEndTime[msg.sender] = block.timestamp + 7 days; // 7 day lock
}

function withdraw(uint256 amount) public {
    require(block.timestamp >= lockEndTime[msg.sender], "Tokens are locked");
    require(stakedAmount[msg.sender] >= amount, "Insufficient staked amount");
    updateRewards(msg.sender);
    stakedAmount[msg.sender] -= amount;
    stakingToken.transfer(msg.sender, amount);
```

```
}
```

Penalty for Early Withdrawal

Introduce a penalty for withdrawals made before the lock period ends.

solidity

```
function withdraw(uint256 amount) public {
    if (block.timestamp < lockEndTime[msg.sender]) {
        uint256 penalty = (amount * 10) / 100; // 10% penalty
        amount -= penalty;
        stakingToken.transfer(owner(), penalty);
    }
    require(stakedAmount[msg.sender] >= amount, "Insufficient
staked amount");
    updateRewards(msg.sender);
    stakedAmount[msg.sender] -= amount;
    stakingToken.transfer(msg.sender, amount);
}
```

Support for Multiple Tokens

To allow staking with different types of tokens, use a mapping to track the balances of each token.

solidity

```
mapping(address => mapping(address => uint256)) public
stakedBalances;

function stake(address token, uint256 amount) public {
    require(amount > 0, "Amount must be greater than 0");
    IERC20(token).transferFrom(msg.sender, address(this),
amount);
```

```
    stakedBalances[token][msg.sender] += amount;
}

function withdraw(address token, uint256 amount) public {
    require(stakedBalances[token][msg.sender] >= amount,
"Insufficient balance");
    stakedBalances[token][msg.sender] -= amount;
    IERC20(token).transfer(msg.sender, amount);
}
```

Testing the Staking Contract

Use tools like **Today** to create and run tests that validate the behavior of the contract.

Staking and Rewards Test

javascript

```javascript
const { expect } = require("chai");

describe("SimpleStaking", function () {
    let stakingToken, rewardToken, stakingContract, owner, user;

    beforeEach(async function () {
        const Token = await
ethers.getContractFactory("ERC20Mock");
        stakingToken = await Token.deploy("StakingToken",
"STK");
        rewardToken = await Token.deploy("RewardToken",
"RWD");
        await stakingToken.mint(owner.address, 10000);
        await rewardToken.mint(owner.address, 5000);
```

```
        const Staking = await
ethers.getContractFactory("SimpleStaking");
        stakingContract = await Staking.deploy(
            stakingToken.address,
            rewardToken.address,
            1 // Reward per second
        );

        [owner, user] = await ethers.getSigners();
    });

    it("should allow users to stake tokens", async function () {
        await
stakingToken.connect(owner).transfer(user.address, 100);
        await
stakingToken.connect(user).approve(stakingContract.address,
100);
        await stakingContract.connect(user).stake(100);

        expect(await
stakingContract.stakedAmount(user.address)).to.equal(100);
    });

    it("should calculate rewards correctly", async function () {
        await
stakingToken.connect(owner).transfer(user.address, 100);
        await
stakingToken.connect(user).approve(stakingContract.address,
100);
        await stakingContract.connect(user).stake(100);

        await ethers.provider.send("evm_increaseTime",
[3600]); // Fast forward 1 hour
        await ethers.provider.send("evm_mine");

        const rewards = await
```

```
stakingContract.rewardDebt(user.address);
    expect(rewards).to.equal(3600);
  });
});
```

Security in Staking Contracts

1. **Indentation Prevention**: Use modifier nonReentrant to avoid attacks.
2. **Data Validation**: Make sure the values submitted are valid before processing them.
3. **Rewards Limits**: Implement limits to avoid excessive issuance of rewards.
4. **Code Audit**: Subject the contract to regular audits to ensure its integrity.

Staking Applications

1. **Proof-of-Stake (PoS)**: Blockchain networks that use staking to validate transactions.
2. **Decentralized Finance (DeFi)**: Liquidity pools that reward users for providing assets.
3. **Loyalty Programs**: Token rewards for customers who participate in long-term programs.
4. **Blockchain Games**: Incentives for players who hold tokens or assets in the game.

Creating staking contracts is an essential skill in developing modern blockchain applications. By implementing efficient and secure contracts, developers can create incentive systems that engage users, promote liquidity, and sustain the network. The use of best practices, such as accurate reward calculations and security mechanisms, ensures the trust and longevity of these decentralized solutions.

CHAPTER 22. REAL USE CASES

Smart contracts have revolutionized several sectors by offering decentralized, secure and programmable solutions to traditional problems. From finance to logistics and governance, they play a crucial role in digitizing processes and creating new business models. This chapter presents real use cases of smart contracts used in the market, detailing how they work, their applications and the codes that support these innovations.

1. Contracts for Decentralized Finance (DeFi)

DeFi protocols have democratized access to financial services, allowing users to borrow, trade and earn without intermediaries.

Liquidity Pools

A liquidity pool allows users to supply tokens to a contract in exchange for a portion of the fees generated from trades.

Simple Liquidity Contract

solidity

```solidity
// SPDX-License-Identifier: MIT
pragma solidity ^0.8.0;

import "@openzeppelin/contracts/token/ERC20/IERC20.sol";

contract LiquidityPool {
    IERC20 public tokenA;
```

```solidity
    IERC20 public tokenB;
    uint256 public totalLiquidityA;
    uint256 public totalLiquidityB;

    constructor(address _tokenA, address _tokenB) {
        tokenA = IERC20(_tokenA);
        tokenB = IERC20(_tokenB);
    }

    function addLiquidity(uint256 amountA, uint256 amountB)
public {
        tokenA.transferFrom(msg.sender, address(this),
amountA);
        tokenB.transferFrom(msg.sender, address(this),
amountB);
        totalLiquidityA += amountA;
        totalLiquidityB += amountB;
    }

    function removeLiquidity(uint256 amountA, uint256
amountB) public {
        require(totalLiquidityA >= amountA && totalLiquidityB
>= amountB, "Insufficient liquidity");
        totalLiquidityA -= amountA;
        totalLiquidityB -= amountB;
        tokenA.transfer(msg.sender, amountA);
        tokenB.transfer(msg.sender, amountB);
    }
}
```

Collateralized Loans

Platforms like Aave and Compound use smart contracts to offer collateralized loans.

Collateralized Loan Agreement

solidity

```solidity
// SPDX-License-Identifier: MIT
pragma solidity ^0.8.0;

import "@openzeppelin/contracts/token/ERC20/IERC20.sol";

contract CollateralizedLoan {
    IERC20 public collateralToken;
    IERC20 public loanToken;
    uint256 public collateralRatio; // in percentage, like 150%

    mapping(address => uint256) public collateralDeposited;
    mapping(address => uint256) public loansTaken;

    constructor(address _collateralToken, address _loanToken,
uint256 _collateralRatio) {
        collateralToken = IERC20(_collateralToken);
        loanToken = IERC20(_loanToken);
        collateralRatio = _collateralRatio;
    }

    function depositCollateral(uint256 amount) public {
        collateralToken.transferFrom(msg.sender, address(this),
amount);
        collateralDeposited[msg.sender] += amount;
    }

    function takeLoan(uint256 amount) public {
        uint256 requiredCollateral = (amount * collateralRatio) /
100;
        require(collateralDeposited[msg.sender] >=
requiredCollateral, "Insufficient collateral");
        loansTaken[msg.sender] += amount;
        loanToken.transfer(msg.sender, amount);
    }

    function repayLoan(uint256 amount) public {
```

```solidity
    require(loansTaken[msg.sender] >= amount, "Loan
amount exceeded");
    loanToken.transferFrom(msg.sender, address(this),
amount);
    loansTaken[msg.sender] -= amount;
  }

  function withdrawCollateral(uint256 amount) public {
    require(collateralDeposited[msg.sender]    >=    amount,
"Insufficient collateral");
    uint256 outstandingLoan = loansTaken[msg.sender];
    uint256    requiredCollateral    =    (outstandingLoan    *
collateralRatio) / 100;
    require(collateralDeposited[msg.sender]  -  amount  >=
requiredCollateral, "Collateral locked");
    collateralDeposited[msg.sender] -= amount;
    collateralToken.transfer(msg.sender, amount);
  }
}
```

2. Contracts for NFTs and Creative Economy

NFTs have transformed the art, music and gaming markets, enabling the creation of unique digital assets.

NFT Marketplace

A marketplace allows the buying and selling of NFTs through smart contracts.

Simple Marketplace Agreement

solidity

```solidity
// SPDX-License-Identifier: MIT
pragma solidity ^0.8.0;

import "@openzeppelin/contracts/token/ERC721/
IERC721.sol";

contract NFTMarketplace {
    struct Listing {
        address seller;
        uint256 price;
    }

    mapping(address => mapping(uint256 => Listing)) public
listings;

    function listNFT(address nftContract, uint256 tokenId,
uint256 price) public {
        IERC721 nft = IERC721(nftContract);
        require(nft.ownerOf(tokenId) == msg.sender, "Not the
owner");
        require(nft.isApprovedForAll(msg.sender, address(this)),
"Marketplace not approved");
        listings[nftContract][tokenId] = Listing(msg.sender,
price);
    }

    function buyNFT(address nftContract, uint256 tokenId)
public payable {
        Listing memory listing = listings[nftContract][tokenId];
        require(msg.value >= listing.price, "Insufficient funds");
        delete listings[nftContract][tokenId];
        payable(listing.seller).transfer(msg.value);
        IERC721(nftContract).safeTransferFrom(listing.seller,
msg.sender, tokenId);
    }
}
```

3. Contracts for Decentralized Governance

Decentralized governance allows communities to make collective decisions about projects and protocols.

Governance DAO

Decentralized Autonomous Organizations (DAOs) use contracts to manage proposals and votes.

DAO contract

solidity

```
// SPDX-License-Identifier: MIT
pragma solidity ^0.8.0;

contract GovernanceDAO {
    struct Proposal {
        string description;
        uint256 voteCount;
        uint256 endTime;
        bool executed;
    }

    Proposal[] public proposals;
    mapping(address => uint256) public votingPower;
    mapping(uint256 => mapping(address => bool)) public
hasVoted;

    function createProposal(string memory description, uint256
duration) public {
        proposals.push(Proposal(description, 0, block.timestamp
+ duration, false));
```

```
    }

    function vote(uint256 proposalId) public {
        require(block.timestamp <
proposals[proposalId].endTime, "Voting ended");
        require(!hasVoted[proposalId][msg.sender], "Already
voted");
        proposals[proposalId].voteCount +=
votingPower[msg.sender];
        hasVoted[proposalId][msg.sender] = true;
    }

    function executeProposal(uint256 proposalId) public {
        Proposal storage proposal = proposals[proposalId];
        require(!proposal.executed, "Already executed");
        require(block.timestamp > proposal.endTime, "Voting still
ongoing");
        proposal.executed = true;
        // Logic to implement the proposal
    }

    function allocateVotingPower(address member, uint256
power) public {
        votingPower[member] += power;
    }
}
```

4. Contracts for Logistics and Supply Chain

Blockchain can track goods, ensuring transparency and authenticity.

Product Tracking

A smart contract can record and track products in a supply chain.

Tracking Contract

solidity

```solidity
// SPDX-License-Identifier: MIT
pragma solidity ^0.8.0;

contract SupplyChain {
    struct Product {
        string name;
        address owner;
        uint256 timestamp;
    }

    mapping(uint256 => Product) public products;

    function registerProduct(uint256 productId, string memory
name) public {
        products[productId] = Product(name, msg.sender,
block.timestamp);
    }

    function transferProduct(uint256 productId, address
newOwner) public {
        require(products[productId].owner == msg.sender, "Not
the owner");
        products[productId].owner = newOwner;
        products[productId].timestamp = block.timestamp;
    }
}
```

Real Applications and Impact

1. **Uniswap**: Automation of token swaps without intermediaries.
2. **OpenSea**: Buying and selling NFTs with marketplace

contracts.
3. **MakerDAO**: Issuance of stablecoins collateralized in cryptoassets.
4. **VeChain**: Tracking global supply chains.

The real-world use cases presented in this chapter demonstrate the versatility and impact of smart contracts across multiple industries. From decentralized finance to governance and logistics, these applications are transforming markets and creating new opportunities. Mastery of these concepts and the ability to implement practical solutions are fundamental skills for any blockchain developer who wants to innovate and lead in the current scenario.

CHAPTER 23. FUTURE OF SOLIDITY

The Solidity language has been the main engine behind the growth and evolution of the Ethereum blockchain. With its ability to create highly programmable smart contracts, it has become indispensable for developers building decentralized solutions. However, as the blockchain ecosystem continues to mature, Solidity faces new challenges and opportunities that will shape its future. This chapter explores emerging trends in language, technological advances, and how Solidity is adapting to meet the demands of a rapidly evolving industry.

1. Evolution of Language

The Solidity development team continues to release regular updates that improve the language's security, efficiency, and usability. These changes aim to meet the needs of developers while addressing the technical challenges of more complex smart contracts.

New Features Planned

1. **More Robust Access Control**:
   - Implementation of native modifiers for access control patterns such as whitelists and administrative roles.
2. **On-chain Resource Management**:
   - Better integration with decentralized storage systems such as IPFS and Filecoin.

3. **Native Support for Multiple Subscriptions**:
   o Facilitation of contracts that require multiple signatures to approve transactions or changes.
4. **Asynchronous Function Execution**:
   o Improved interoperability between contracts that require asynchronous responses, eliminating the need for manual calls between contracts.

Security Improvements

Security is a fundamental aspect of Solidity's design. Recent and upcoming updates address the most common vulnerabilities, such as undercutting and gas overload.

Native Recess Pattern

With the introduction of automatic reentrancy protections, contracts can block malicious attempts without relying on external libraries:

solidity

```solidity
contract SecureContract {
    bool private locked;

    modifier noReentrant() {
        require(!locked, "No reentrant calls");
        locked = true;
        _;
        locked = false;
    }

    function withdraw(uint256 amount) public noReentrant {
        // safe withdrawal logic
    }
}
```

2. Emerging Trends

Modularity and Composition

Creating modular contracts is becoming common practice, allowing developers to compose complex systems from smaller, reusable components.

Modularity with Libraries

Libraries play an important role in modular design. They allow the reuse of functions and reduce implementation costs:

solidity

```solidity
library Math {
    function add(uint256 a, uint256 b) internal pure returns
(uint256) {
        return a + b;
    }

    function multiply(uint256 a, uint256 b) internal pure
returns (uint256) {
        return a * b;
    }
}

contract ModularContract {
    using Math for uint256;

    function calculate(uint256 a, uint256 b) public pure returns
(uint256) {
        return a.add(b).multiply(2);
    }
}
```

Upgradable Contracts

The demand for contracts that can be updated without the need for frequent deployments has led to the development of standards such as **proxy patterns**. These techniques are evolving to offer greater flexibility and security.

Proxy Pattern Implementation

solidity

```
contract Proxy {
    address public implementation;

    function setImplementation(address newImplementation)
public {
        implementation = newImplementation;
    }

    fallback() external payable {
        (bool success, ) = implementation.delegatecall(msg.data);
        require(success, "Delegatecall failed");
    }
}
```

Interoperability with Other Blockchains

With the growth of blockchains like Polkadot, Avalanche, and Binance Smart Chain, interoperability between networks is becoming essential. Solidity is evolving to support multi-chain contracts.

3. Technological Challenges

Scalability

With the increasing adoption of Ethereum, scalability has become one of the biggest challenges. The introduction of Ethereum 2.0 and **sharding** presents new paradigms for Solidity developers.

Contracts Optimized for Rollups

Rollups, such as zk-Rollups and optimistic rollups, allow you to process transactions outside the main chain, reducing gas consumption:

solidity

```solidity
contract RollupContract {
    mapping(address => uint256) public balances;

    function deposit(uint256 amount) public {
        balances[msg.sender] += amount;
        // off-chain processing logic
    }
}
```

Sustainability

The environmental sustainability of blockchain is a growing concern. With the move to proof-of-stake (PoS), Solidity needs to adapt to energy-efficient consensus models.

4. Adaptations for New Uses

Smart Contracts for IoT

Integrating IoT devices with blockchain is creating new use cases such as home automation and supply chain management.

Example of Automation with IoT

solidity

```solidity
contract IoTDeviceManager {
    mapping(address => bool) public authorizedDevices;

    function registerDevice(address device) public {
        authorizedDevices[device] = true;
    }

    function executeCommand(address device, string memory
command) public view returns (string memory) {
        require(authorizedDevices[device], "Device not
authorized");
        // command execution logic
        return command;
    }
}
```

Contracts Based on Artificial Intelligence

AI-based solutions are being integrated with contracts for decisions based on machine learning and predictive models.

Contracts that Use AI via Oracles

solidity

```solidity
interface IAIOracle {
    function getPrediction(string memory data) external view
returns (uint256);
}

contract AIIntegration {
    IAIOracle public oracle;
```

```solidity
constructor(address oracleAddress) {
    oracle = IAIOracle(oracleAddress);
}

function getMarketPrediction(string memory marketData)
public view returns (uint256) {
    return oracle.getPrediction(marketData);
}
}
```

5. Tools and Ecosystem

Solidity's evolution also depends on tools that support contract development, auditing, and testing.

Emerging Tools

1. **Slither**: Static analysis to identify vulnerabilities.
2. **Today**: Development framework with advanced support for testing and deployment.
3. **Foundry**: Quick tool for contract testing and benchmarking.

6. Adoption of Standards

With the introduction of new standards such as ERC-721 for NFTs and ERC-4626 for yield vaults, standardization remains a priority to ensure interoperability.

ERC-4626 Implementation Example

solidity

```solidity
import "@openzeppelin/contracts/token/ERC20/ERC20.sol";
```

```
import "@openzeppelin/contracts/token/ERC20/extensions/
ERC4626.sol";

contract YieldVault is ERC4626 {
    constructor(address asset) ERC4626(ERC20(asset))
ERC20("YieldVault", "YV") {}
}
```

The future of Solidity is promising and challenging. The language is adapting to technological changes, introducing new features, addressing scalability and security issues, and exploring new frontiers like IoT and AI. By keeping up with trends and innovations, developers can create more robust and innovative solutions, strengthening blockchain's impact on the world. Solidity will continue to be a driving force in advancing the decentralized ecosystem, shaping the next generation of applications and smart contracts.

CHAPTER 24. COMPLETE PRACTICAL EXAMPLE

In this chapter, a functional project will be developed using Solidity, integrating the concepts explored previously in the book. The goal is to build a complete decentralized application (dApp) that includes well-designed smart contracts, token interaction, and practical use case support. The chosen project will be a **decentralized crowdfunding**, where users can create campaigns, contribute funds and withdraw the amounts collected after reaching the goal.

This project incorporates elements such as security, fund management, monitoring events and a clear interface for participants.

1. Project Description

Main Features

1. **Campaign Creation**:
   o   An organizer can create a campaign with a defined fundraising goal and deadline.
2. **Contributions**:
   o   Any user can contribute to an active campaign by sending Ether.
3. **Monitoring**:
   o   Full transparency for users to track campaign

progress.
4. **Closing and Withdrawal**:
   o   The organizer can end the campaign and withdraw the funds if the goal is reached. Otherwise, contributors may withdraw their amounts.

Requirements

1. **Security**:
   o   Ensure that funds are managed reliably and that vulnerabilities such as re-entrants do not occur.
2. **Performance**:
   o   Efficiency in the use of gas.
3. **Usability**:
   o   Clear and accessible information for organizers and contributors.

---

2. Contract Development

Contract Structure

The main contract manages the campaigns and their interactions. Below is the contract code with explanations of each functionality.

solidity

```solidity
// SPDX-License-Identifier: MIT
pragma solidity ^0.8.0;

contract DecentralizedCrowdfunding {
    struct Campaign {
        address organizer;
        string description;
```

```solidity
        uint256 goalAmount;
        uint256 deadline;
        uint256 totalFunds;
        bool completed;
        mapping(address => uint256) contributions;
    }

    uint256 public campaignCount;
    mapping(uint256 => Campaign) public campaigns;

    event CampaignCreated(uint256 indexed campaignId,
address indexed organizer, uint256 goalAmount, uint256
deadline);
    event ContributionReceived(uint256 indexed campaignId,
address indexed contributor, uint256 amount);
    event CampaignCompleted(uint256 indexed campaignId,
uint256 totalFunds);
    event RefundIssued(uint256 indexed campaignId, address
indexed contributor, uint256 amount);

    modifier onlyOrganizer(uint256 campaignId) {
        require(msg.sender == campaigns[campaignId].organizer,
"Not the campaign organizer");
        _;
    }

    modifier campaignActive(uint256 campaignId) {
        require(block.timestamp <=
campaigns[campaignId].deadline, "Campaign has ended");
        require(!campaigns[campaignId].completed, "Campaign
already completed");
        _;
    }

    function createCampaign(string memory description,
uint256 goalAmount, uint256 duration) public {
        require(goalAmount > 0, "Goal amount must be greater
```

than zero");
    require(duration > 0, "Duration must be greater than zero");

    campaignCount++;
    Campaign storage newCampaign = campaigns[campaignCount];
    newCampaign.organizer = msg.sender;
    newCampaign.description = description;
    newCampaign.goalAmount = goalAmount;
    newCampaign.deadline = block.timestamp + duration;

    emit CampaignCreated(campaignCount, msg.sender, goalAmount, newCampaign.deadline);
  }

  function contribute(uint256 campaignId) public payable campaignActive(campaignId) {
    require(msg.value > 0, "Contribution must be greater than zero");

    Campaign storage campaign = campaigns[campaignId];
    campaign.contributions[msg.sender] += msg.value;
    campaign.totalFunds += msg.value;

    emit ContributionReceived(campaignId, msg.sender, msg.value);
  }

  function withdrawFunds(uint256 campaignId) public onlyOrganizer(campaignId) {
    Campaign storage campaign = campaigns[campaignId];
    require(block.timestamp > campaign.deadline, "Campaign is still active");
    require(campaign.totalFunds >= campaign.goalAmount, "Goal not reached");

```solidity
        campaign.completed = true;
        payable(campaign.organizer).transfer(campaign.totalFun
ds);

        emit CampaignCompleted(campaignId,
campaign.totalFunds);
    }

    function requestRefund(uint256 campaignId) public {
        Campaign storage campaign = campaigns[campaignId];
        require(block.timestamp > campaign.deadline, "Campaign
is still active");
        require(campaign.totalFunds < campaign.goalAmount,
"Goal reached, refunds not allowed");

        uint256 contribution =
campaign.contributions[msg.sender];
        require(contribution > 0, "No contributions to refund");

        campaign.contributions[msg.sender] = 0;
        payable(msg.sender).transfer(contribution);

        emit RefundIssued(campaignId, msg.sender,
contribution);
    }

    function getCampaignDetails(uint256 campaignId) public
view returns (
        address organizer,
        string memory description,
        uint256 goalAmount,
        uint256 deadline,
        uint256 totalFunds,
        bool completed
    ) {
        Campaign storage campaign = campaigns[campaignId];
```

```
    return (
        campaign.organizer,
        campaign.description,
        campaign.goalAmount,
        campaign.deadline,
        campaign.totalFunds,
        campaign.completed
    );
  }
}
```

---

3. Explanation of the Code

1. **Data Structure**:
   - The structure Campaign stores essential information about each campaign, including the organizer, goal, deadline, funds raised and a mapping of contributions by user.

2. **Campaign Creation**:
   - createCampaign allows an organizer to register a new campaign, defining the description, goal and duration.

3. **Contributions**:
   - contribute allows users to send Ether to an active campaign, updating total funds and their individual contributions.

4. **Withdrawals by the Organizer**:
   - withdrawFunds allows the organizer to withdraw the funds raised after the deadline, as long as the goal has been reached.

5. **Refunds**:
   - requestRefund ensures that taxpayers can recover their amounts if the campaign goal is not reached within the deadline.

6. **Events**:
   o   Events are issued to record significant actions such as campaign creation, contributions received, campaign completions, and refunds processed.

4. Testing the Contract

Automated Tests with Hardhat

Below is a test script to validate the contract functionalities.

javascript

```javascript
const { expect } = require("chai");

describe("DecentralizedCrowdfunding", function () {
   let Crowdfunding, crowdfunding, owner, contributor1,
contributor2;

   beforeEach(async function () {
      Crowdfunding = await
ethers.getContractFactory("DecentralizedCrowdfunding");
      [owner, contributor1, contributor2] = await
ethers.getSigners();
      crowdfunding = await Crowdfunding.deploy();
   });

   it("should allow creating a campaign", async function () {
      await crowdfunding.createCampaign("Test Campaign",
ethers.utils.parseEther("10"), 3600);
      const campaignDetails = await
crowdfunding.getCampaignDetails(1);
      expect(campaignDetails.goalAmount).to.equal(ethers.util
s.parseEther("10"));
   });
```

```
    it("should allow contributions to a campaign", async
function () {
        await crowdfunding.createCampaign("Test Campaign",
ethers.utils.parseEther("10"), 3600);
        await crowdfunding.connect(contributor1).contribute(1,
{ value: ethers.utils.parseEther("1") });
        const campaignDetails = await
crowdfunding.getCampaignDetails(1);
        expect(campaignDetails.totalFunds).to.equal(ethers.utils.
parseEther("1"));
    });

    it("should allow organizer to withdraw funds if goal is
reached", async function () {
        await crowdfunding.createCampaign("Test Campaign",
ethers.utils.parseEther("10"), 1);
        await crowdfunding.connect(contributor1).contribute(1,
{ value: ethers.utils.parseEther("10") });
        await ethers.provider.send("evm_increaseTime", [3600]);
        await crowdfunding.withdrawFunds(1);
    });

    it("should allow contributors to request refunds if goal is not
reached", async function () {
        await crowdfunding.createCampaign("Test Campaign",
ethers.utils.parseEther("10"), 1);
        await crowdfunding.connect(contributor1).contribute(1,
{ value: ethers.utils.parseEther("1") });
        await ethers.provider.send("evm_increaseTime", [3600]);
        await
crowdfunding.connect(contributor1).requestRefund(1);
    });
});
```

5. Applications and Expansions

1. **Reward Tokens**:
   - Add token rewards for contributors.
2. **Integration with NFTs**:
   - Create NFTs as recognition for large donors.
3. **Analytics**:
   - Add detailed metrics about campaigns, such as success rates.

The decentralized crowdfunding contract demonstrates how fundamental concepts can be applied to solve real-world problems in an innovative and efficient way. With security, transparency and scalability as central pillars, this project exemplifies the power of smart contracts in creating disruptive solutions. Developers can use this foundation to build more sophisticated systems, adding functionality and customizations as needed.

CHAPTER 25. ADVANCED TIPS AND RESOURCES

Developing smart contracts with Solidity requires not only a solid technical understanding, but also the application of best practices to ensure efficiency, security, and ease of maintenance. This chapter covers advanced tips for developers, highlighting techniques that help you create robust, optimized contracts. Additionally, it explores available resources and communities for continuous learning, emphasizing tools, open source platforms, and discussion forums.

1. Best Practices in Development with Solidity

Security as a Priority

Security is one of the most critical aspects in developing smart contracts. An error in the code can result in significant financial losses and reputational damage.

Indentation Prevention:

- Always update the state before transferring funds to avoid reentrancy attacks.

solidity

```
bool private locked;

modifier noReentrant() {
   require(!locked, "Reentrant call");
```

```solidity
    locked = true;
    _;
    locked = false;
}

function withdraw(uint256 amount) public noReentrant {
    require(balances[msg.sender]  >=  amount, "Insufficient
balance");
    balances[msg.sender] -= amount;
    payable(msg.sender).transfer(amount);
}
```

Access Limitation:

- o   Implement tight controls for sensitive functions using modifiers.

solidity

```solidity
address public owner;

modifier onlyOwner() {
    require(msg.sender == owner, "Not the owner");
    _;
}

function setNewOwner(address newOwner) public onlyOwner
{
    owner = newOwner;
}
```

Input Validation:

- o   Check all entries to avoid unexpected behavior.

solidity

```
function setThreshold(uint256 newThreshold) public {
    require(newThreshold > 0, "Threshold must be positive");
    threshold = newThreshold;
}
```

Rigorous Testing:

- ○ Write comprehensive tests that cover edge cases and unlikely scenarios.

Gas Optimization

Contracts that consume less gas are more economical and efficient. Optimizing gas consumption is essential to keep costs low for users.

Use Appropriate Data Types:

- ○ Prefer types like uint8 or uint16 for variables that do not require the full space of a uint256.

solidity

uint8 smallValue; // More gas efficient

Minimize Storage Usage:

- ○ Reduce the number of reads and writes to storage.

solidity

uint256 private cachedValue;

```solidity
function calculate() public view returns (uint256) {
    return cachedValue * 2; // Avoid unnecessary readings
}
```

Avoid Unnecessary Loops:

- o   Whenever possible, replace loops with straightforward batch operations.

solidity

```solidity
function batchProcess(address[] memory accounts, uint256 amount) public {
    for (uint256 i = 0; i < accounts.length; i++) {
        balances[accounts[i]] += amount;
    }
}
```

Prefer Events to Storage:

- o   Use events to record actions instead of storing data permanently.

solidity

```solidity
event ActionLogged(address indexed user, uint256 value);

function performAction(uint256 value) public {
    emit ActionLogged(msg.sender, value);
}
```

Modularity and Reusability

Designing modular contracts makes code easier to maintain and update. Reusing functions and libraries also reduces the cost of development and execution.

Use Libraries:

- Take advantage of external libraries, like those from OpenZeppelin, to avoid reinventing the wheel.

solidity

```solidity
import "@openzeppelin/contracts/math/SafeMath.sol";

library MyLibrary {
    function add(uint256 a, uint256 b) internal pure returns (uint256) {
        return a + b;
    }
}
```

Split Large Contracts:

- Break large contracts into smaller modules that interact with each other.

solidity

```solidity
contract Token {
    // Token logic
}

contract Marketplace {
    // Market logic
}
```

2. Essential Resources

Development Tools

1. **Remix IDE:**
   o A browser-based platform for developing, testing and deploying smart contracts. Includes gas debugging and analysis.
2. **Today:**
   o Advanced framework for local development, including support for testing, simulations and deployment scripts.
3. **Foundry:**
   o Modern tool for developing and testing Solidity contracts, known for its speed.
4. **Slither:**
   o Static analysis tool that identifies vulnerabilities in Solidity contracts.
5. **Tenderly:**
   o Platform that offers debugging, monitoring and simulation of transactions in real time.

Open Source Platforms

1. **OpenZeppelin:**
   o Industry standard smart contract library. Includes implementations of ERC-20, ERC-721, and security modules.
2. **Chain link:**
   o Provides oracles for integration with real-world data and external APIs.
3. **Ethers.js:**

o   JavaScript library for interacting with Ethereum contracts.

4. **Web3.js:**

o   Widely used library for dApp development.

Communities and Forums

1. **Ethereum Stack Exchange:**

o   Forum for technical questions related to Ethereum and Solidity.

2. **Discord do Ethereum:**

o   Space for discussions between developers and updates from the Ethereum community.

3. **Reddit: r/ethdev:**

o   Ethereum developer community where projects and ideas are shared.

4. **GitHub:**

o   Explore popular Solidity repositories to learn best practices and collaborate with other developers.

---

3. Advanced Tips for Continuous Development

Monitoring and Auditing

Automate Audits:

o   Use tools like MythX and Slither for automated security analysis.

Record Important Activities:

o   Use events to track critical actions in the contract.

solidity

```solidity
event OwnershipTransferred(address indexed previousOwner,
address indexed newOwner);

function    transferOwnership(address    newOwner)    public
onlyOwner {
    emit OwnershipTransferred(owner, newOwner);
    owner = newOwner;
}
```

Gradual Implementation:

o   Deploy contracts on test networks before moving them to production.

Continuous Learning

1. **Track Solidity Updates**:
o   Constantly review the release notes to stay up to date with new features.
2. **Contribute to Open Source Projects**:
o   Joining existing projects is a great way to learn from experienced developers.
3. **Hackathons and Contests**:
o   Participate in blockchain-related hackathons to improve practical skills.

4. Practical Case: Application of Tips

Scenario: Creating a Secure and Optimized ERC-20 Token

Code:

solidity

```solidity
// SPDX-License-Identifier: MIT
pragma solidity ^0.8.0;

import "@openzeppelin/contracts/token/ERC20/ERC20.sol";
import "@openzeppelin/contracts/access/Ownable.sol";

contract MyToken is ERC20, Ownable {
    constructor() ERC20("MyToken", "MTK") {
        _mint(msg.sender, 1000000 * 10**decimals());
    }

    function burn(uint256 amount) public onlyOwner {
        _burn(msg.sender, amount);
    }

    function mint(address to, uint256 amount) public
onlyOwner {
        _mint(to, amount);
    }
}
```

Applied Tips:

1. **Uso de OpenZeppelin**:
   o   Avoid errors by reusing tested and audited contracts.
2. **Access Control**:
   o   Ownable protects sensitive functions.
3. **Efficiency**:
   o   Simple and optimized operations to minimize gas consumption.

Developing smart contracts in Solidity requires attention to detail, application of best practices, and use of modern tools. By following the advanced tips presented and taking advantage of community resources, developers can create efficient, secure, and scalable contracts. Continuous learning is essential to stay up to date with rapid changes in the blockchain ecosystem, ensuring robust solutions for future challenges.

FINAL CONCLUSION

The evolution of blockchain represents one of the most profound transformations in the digital world in recent decades. From its initial conception with Bitcoin to the vast ecosystem we have today, blockchain has transcended its original function of recording financial transactions to become the foundation of innovations in decentralized finance, governance, supply chains, and more. Solidity, as one of the fundamental programming languages for smart contracts, has played an essential role in this journey, enabling revolutionary ideas to be transformed into practical realities.

Solidity's impact on blockchain is not limited to contract programming; is the language that allows you to automate processes, remove intermediaries and create trust in a decentralized environment. With its ability to handle complex logic and interact with different systems, Solidity has driven the creation of decentralized applications (dApps) that are reshaping industries. This book covered all aspects necessary to master this language, from the fundamentals to creating advanced solutions. Throughout the chapters, we present concepts, techniques and best practices to enable developers to innovate and contribute significantly to the blockchain ecosystem.

Chapter Summary

Chapter 1: Introduction to Solidity

The journey began with an overview of the Solidity language, its importance in the blockchain ecosystem and its practical applications. The chapter highlighted how the language has become the standard for developing smart contracts on Ethereum and other supported platforms.

Chapter 2: Configuring the Development Environment

Setting up an efficient development environment is essential. This chapter detailed fundamental tools such as Remix, Truffle, and Hardhat, as well as guidance for setting up on-premises and cloud environments.

Chapter 3: Fundamentals of Solidity

The fundamentals were explored with a focus on the basic structure of a smart contract. We discuss data types, variables, and visibility modifiers, laying the foundation for more complex contracts.

Chapter 4: Functions in Solidity

In this chapter, we delve into role creation, structure, and best practices. We differentiate the functions view, pure and payable, providing detailed examples for each case.

Chapter 5: Flow Control and Loops

We discuss the use of control structures like if/else, while and for. The chapter highlighted how loops can be used efficiently and safely.

Chapter 6: Events and Logs

Events are crucial for transparency in smart contracts. This chapter explained how to record actions on the blockchain and monitor important events.

Chapter 7: Arrays and Mappings

We cover the creation and manipulation of arrays and mappings, essential data structures for smart contracts that require information storage and retrieval.

Chapter 8: Structures and Enums

The creation of custom structures and the use of enums were explored as tools to represent states and organize data efficiently.

Chapter 9: Modifiers and Inheritance

This chapter highlighted the use of custom modifiers for access control and inheritance for code reuse in contracts.

Chapter 10: Payments and Transfers

Focusing on Ether, we address the differences between send, transfer and call, explaining how to handle payments securely.

Chapter 11: Security in Smart Contracts

Security was explored in depth, with a focus on protecting against reentrancy, overflow, and other common vulnerabilities.

Chapter 12: Testing Contracts

Automated testing was discussed using frameworks like Hardhat. We highlight the importance of ensuring contracts work as expected.

Chapter 13: Contract Deployment

We cover the process of deploying contracts on testnets and mainnets, including interaction with tools like MetaMask.

Chapter 14: Interacting with dApps

The integration of smart contracts with frontend interfaces was explored, using libraries such as Web3.js and Ethers.js.

Chapter 15: ERC-20: Creating Fungible Tokens

We introduce the ERC-20 standard, explaining how to create fungible tokens with essential functions such as transfer and approve.

Chapter 16: ERC-721: Creating NFTs

We explore the ERC-721 standard for creating NFTs, highlighting its uses in digital art, gaming, and intellectual property.

Chapter 17: ERC-1155: Multimodality Tokens

This chapter detailed the ERC-1155 standard, which allows you to efficiently create fungible and non-fungible tokens.

Chapter 18: Complex Contracts and DAO

We have developed more advanced contracts and introduced Decentralized Autonomous Organizations (DAOs) for decentralized governance.

Chapter 19: Contract Interoperability

We discuss how smart contracts can interact with each other and with external APIs, using oracles to access off-chain data.

Chapter 20: Gas Optimization

The reduction of execution costs was addressed, with strategies to optimize gas consumption in contracts.

Chapter 21: Staking Contracts

We develop contracts for staking and rewards systems, exploring their importance in the DeFi ecosystem.

Chapter 22: Real Use Cases

Practical examples demonstrated how smart contracts are used in markets, decentralized finance and governance.

Chapter 23: Future of Solidity

We explore emerging trends in language and how it is adapting to new technological challenges.

Chapter 24: Complete Practical Example

We have developed a complete working project, showing the creation of a decentralized crowdfunding system from scratch.

Chapter 25: Advanced Tips and Resources

We finish with advanced tips and a list of resources and communities for continued learning.

Thank you for committing to this journey of learning and exploration. Your effort and dedication demonstrate a remarkable commitment to mastering Solidity and contributing to the blockchain ecosystem. We hope this book has provided not only the technical knowledge, but also the inspiration to apply these concepts to real solutions that impact the world.

You are now equipped to turn ideas into innovations and collaborate to shape the future of decentralized technology. Good luck on your journey as a smart contract developer!

Cordially,
Diego Rodrigues & Team!

QR CODE AND ACTIVATION LINK

https://bit.ly/4iTFsFH

Execute. Test. Practice. Transform.

You are not alone — Connect to the GLOBAL Neural Network of Education.

UpAndGo!